Biblical Proof:
Animals *Do* Go To Heaven

Biblical Proof:
Animals *Do* Go To Heaven

By

Steven H. Woodward

XULON PRESS

Xulon Press
2301 Lucien Way #415
Maitland, FL 32751
407.339.4217
www.xulonpress.com

Unless otherwise indicated, Scripture quotations taken from the
King James Version (KJV) – *public domain.*

Printed in the United States of America.

ISBN-13: 978-1-6241-9282-1

Table of Contents

Preface vii
Introduction. ix
Dedication. xv
God Sings to Us xvii

PART I
  1. What God Says About His Animals. 1
  2. Animals Worship God 6
  3. Learning from Animals 13
  4. Spirits and God's Love. 18
  5. God Preserves the Spirits of Animals 25
  6. God Blesses His Animals. 31
  7. God Uses His Animals. 34

PART II
  8. Meeting And Adopting BJ 49
  9. Getting to Know BJ 58
  10. The First Vision 67
  11. The Second Vision 76
  12. My Wife's Dream. 94
  13. Jesus Sends Jasper 97

PART III
  14. King Solomon's Wisdom 107
  15. We Brought Animals Into Sin 111

Epilogue 117
To My Wife. 119
Work Cited 121
About the Author. 123

Preface

The day after my beloved dog BJ passed away my wife saw him in a dream but she did not tell me because she didn't want to upset me. She knew I had been praying to see BJ and asking Jesus to let me know if he was in heaven with Him. And that I had also asked God to let me see him just one more time.

After three weeks of praying, the Lord finally brought BJ to me in a vision. And when I related my vision to my wife, she then told me of her dream. In her dream she described BJ and it was the same description as what I had seen in my vision.

I would like to introduce my dogs to you so you will know them when you read this book. When I was about seven years old my father got me a hound dog, and we named him Duke. He was brown in color and he had a pink nose. He was a puppy and he and I grew up together. He lived to be almost fourteen years of age.

Years later my wife and I got a Boston terrier for our two sons and we named him Petie. He was a long-legged dog and his fur was black and white and he lived to be over fifteen years of age. My two sons grew up with Petie.

And the third dog was named BJ and he came to us by chance, or so we thought, but it was actually God's will which we later came to realize. He was a gray and white Shih Tzu and his age was estimated at about eight years when he came to us. He had been very badly abused and neglected and he died at about age fifteen, but the last six years of his life he lived like a king.

Introduction

"But he knoweth the way that I take: when
he hath tried me, I shall come forth as gold."
-*Job 23:10*

First let me make it perfectly clear that my intent is not to place animals above the redemption of man. Jesus died on the cross for you and me and we need redemption and salvation; animals do not. Men were created with free will and in contrast, animals were born with God given instincts. The fall of man brought all of creation into corruption. We humans corrupted all of God's creation.

I came to Jesus about two years ago and although I had been saved many times throughout my life I never really took it seriously. My reasoning for getting saved was, "just in case" or what some people call "fire insurance". However I have always prayed and talked to God, but I had never heard Him answer me before. I guess I never really took the time to listen, but when I look back on my life I see that I have always been blessed and that Jesus has always been with me.

I was active in the church as a young child and loved to sing in the choir, especially the older hymns. I have always been an open minded person and I have always believed in God and Jesus, however I just didn't believe that Jesus loved me. There is a saying that goes like this, "You may believe in God, but you don't *believe* God." That described me and like most people I thought that I was going to heaven because I was a good person. I didn't realize that I was a sinner and needed salvation and I always thought that Jesus helped everyone else, but not me. All my life I thought that I was on my own.

After being saved something happened to me and I got filled with the spirit and received my first vision in church and I have had many visions since then. (I used to ask men questions about the Bible, now I ask Jesus). I began to pray earnestly to God and He began to talk to me. I prayed every day. I prayed to Jesus the first thing upon waking, I prayed all during the day, and it was the last thing I did before going to bed.

All my life I have heard people ask and wonder what happens to their pets when they die, and so did I. When my dog BJ died I really needed to know the answer to this age old question and his death put me on a quest to learn the answer to this question. And only Jesus could answer that question. I prayed for three weeks constantly until I received an answer. Jesus finally answered me and I am recounting my experiences in this book the best that I can. After my experience, Jesus instructed me to write this book in order to share this knowledge with other people, so that they too would know how great His love is. In my book I will share with you my visions, and the scriptures that the Lord showed me in order to prove that animals do go to heaven. I am quite confident after you read this book, that you will know exactly where your pets are and that you will be confident in knowing that they are in heaven with Jesus, waiting for you. The Lord instructed me that this was His book; not mine.

And that I was simply to write it to the best of my ability. He told me that it would be a very small, but very important word that would bring people to Him. And that it would also draw those that are with Him, much closer. He told me that it would give believers and non believers alike a better understanding of His love.

I know that many people who have lost their beloved pets harbor some resentfulness in their heart towards God, because I know that I did. And they ask themselves, "How could God make animals and then just throw them away; how cruel!"

People love their animals dearly and they want them to be in heaven so that they can spend eternity with them. They think to themselves, "How is it possible that a God, who speaks of love, refuses to give my pet eternal life in heaven?" Jesus wants you to know that He does love them and that they *do* receive eternal life in heaven. And as a matter of fact, if one of your pets has passed on recently or in the past, he or she is waiting for you in heaven right now.

Every creature in this world has a purpose and they maintain the environment, but they also feed and clothe us. Without this we could not exist. They all do certain jobs such as, pollinating, making food, (Honey) and making material (Silk) cleaning the environment, and some are even beasts of burden. Then there are the ones that God made to be *companions and teachers*. These are the animals that we become close to.

I have heard many people say that animals don't have spirits, but this is simply not true, and I intend to prove through the word of God that animals do go to heaven, and that they do have spirits.

This is a story of my experience, but it is also a lesson from Jesus to all of us. He sent a dog named BJ to me in order to teach me about love and forgiveness, and he did it because I asked Him to.

In the first section I will show you indisputable proof with Bible scripture that will help you to understand how the Lord looks upon His animals. There may be some who read this book and think I am silly for loving my pets so much, but I feel sorry for those people because they are missing the greatness of His love. Jesus alone created all things *by* and *through* His love and there is no limit to His love.

In the second section I will tell you of my wife's dream and of my vision where Jesus brought BJ to me; after he had passed. And along with that, he also brought me knowledge, wisdom, understanding, and love. And finally how He brought me another gift named Jasper.

And lastly in the third section I will show you more scriptural proof that animals do go to heaven, and then you can decide for yourself. I hope that God blesses you by reading this book like He did for me.

Dedication

I wish to dedicate this book to God our heavenly Father. I take no credit for this book because it all came from Him. Secondly I dedicate this book to BJ, the anointed dog that God sent to me, in order to teach me about God's great love and unending forgiveness.

And thirdly to my wife who encouraged and supported me and to my two sons and my three grandchildren whom I love dearly.

To Lauren, Nicky, and Liam. I love you so much. Always keep Jesus in your heart.

And a special thanks to Jesse who gave me inspiration when I was having doubts about writing this book. I saw his dog Cooley pulling little Jesse up the hill in his red wagon by a rope. God works in mysterious ways.

God Bless.

God Sings to Us

G od tells us that He made us in His image. So if we laugh, sing, and love, then God also laughs, sings, and loves just as we do. And He loves all of his creation, and this includes animals.

> *"The LORD thy God in the midst of thee is mighty; he will save, he will rejoice over thee with joy, he will rest in His love, He will joy over thee with singing." (Zephaniah 3:17)*

> *"Thou art my hiding place; thou shalt preserve me from trouble; thou shalt compass me about with songs of deliverance. Se-lah." (Psalms 32:7)*

Webster' dictionary defines the word *Image* as: "A physical likeness or representation of a person, *animal,* or thing; counterpart, or copy" (Page 659).

Sign on my dog groomer's door:

"Dogs are little children with furry coats."

"And they brought young children to him, that he should touch them: and his disciples rebuked those that brought them. But when Jesus saw it, he was much displeased, and said unto them, Suffer the little children to come unto me, and forbid them not: for of such is the kingdom of God."

(Mark 10:13-14)

PART I

"The fool hath said in his heart, There is no God." -Psalm 14:1

Chapter 1

What God Says About His Animals

"And God saw every thing that he had made, and behold, it was very good."-Genesis 1:31

First let's establish who made everything and who is responsible for all of creation. The Bible tells us that Jesus created everything and it also tells us that Jesus created everything *for Himself.*

> *"For by him were all things created, that are in heaven, and that are in earth, visible and invisible, whether they be thrones, or dominions, or principalities, or powers: all things were created by him, and for him: And he is before all*

things, and by him all things consist."(Colos-
sians 1:16-17)

In the scripture above, the Apostle Paul states that Jesus created *all* things that are in heaven and earth. And if you notice, Paul repeats this fact twice. He wants us to know that Jesus created all things. And it tells us that everything consists, or depends on Him.

> "And God made the beast of the earth after his kind, and cattle after their kind, and every thing that creepeth upon the earth after his kind: and God saw that it was good." (Genesis 1:25)

> "And God saw every thing that he had made, and behold, it was very good." (Genesis 1:31)

In both of the verses above, God says that everything He created was good...very good. If the Lord God says that everything that He created is very good, then I believe Him with all my heart. I believe that God's meaning of very good is *perfect*.

"The earth is the LORD's, and the fullness thereof; the world, and they that dwell therein."
(Psalm 24:1)

In the verse above, the word *fullness* means everything on earth. Webster's dictionary defines the word *"fullness"* as "complete; entire; maximum" (Page 530). Don't animals dwell here too? Well, of course they do, and doesn't the above scripture say, *"...and they that dwell therein?"* it most certainly does, so now we have established that God made all of creation and that it all belongs to God and Him alone... not us. And if the Lord claims that everything is His, then animals most definitely belong to Him too. And I don't think that Jesus created animals only to throw them away.

In my visions the Lord poured out His wisdom to me and this opened up my eyes to the amazing depth and width of His love. God showed me His love towards all of His creation, whereas before I was like most people, being mainly focused on the human aspect of God's love.

I realize now how egotistical and selfish I had been, thinking only of His love for me and mankind. I realized that being egotistical and closed minded actually limited my understanding of God's immense love, and therefore it was a stumbling block

3

by blinding me to the full scope of God's love. I have heard many people, including Christians and pastors, say that animals don't have spirits, and that they don't go to heaven. I feel sorry for these people because they have closed their minds to the infinite love and mind of Jesus. They are basically saying that the love of Jesus *is limited*.

This limited belief is simply not true because God says differently in His word. If you read the Bible you can see that it tells us that animals do have spirits and that they do go to heaven. The scriptures quoted in this book are God's holy words; not mine, and if you are like me and truly believe what the Bible says, then you will find comfort in the loss of your pet, just as I did. I intend to prove that animals are created, blessed, loved, and preserved (Saved) by God.

Again, I'm not saying that animals are more important than humans, but what I am saying is that it is very important to understand that we are not the only creation of Jesus Christ. And by realizing this fact it will lead you to a deeper understanding of the awesome love of Jesus. I hope my story will bring you closer to God like it did for me and that it brings you a better understanding of the real meaning of God's unconditional love and forgiveness.

I intend to show you that God not only talks to His animals, but that they work for Him, and that He also uses them to teach humans. Through the death of my dog, God made me seek His word more diligently, which caused me to pray harder, and to study His word much closer. God poured out His wisdom and gave me a true understanding of His word. Through His guidance, God showed me the true meaning of the verses that are quoted in this book.

But of course I did what the Bible instructs us to do which is to have a love for the truth. Or in other words, have an open mind, ask, and search.

Chapter 2

Animals Worship God

"Let every thing that hath breath praise the
LORD. Praise ye the LORD. -Psalm 150:6

The Bible tells us that animals worship God and it states this fact throughout the entire book. Look carefully at the verse below because it tells us that all creatures have spirits.

"God is a Spir'-it: and they that worship him must
worship him in spirit and in truth." (John 4:24)

The above scripture states that *God is a spirit* and only those that have spirits are able to worship Him. This proves without a doubt that animals do have spirits because they would not be able to worship God without a spirit. God says that you *can not* worship Him unless you are in the spirit and this means that you have to *have* a spirit, in order to be *in* the spirit, in order to worship Him.

So now we know that animals have spirits just like we do, only they are different spirits than ours, due to the fact that every spirit is different. Your spirit is not the same as my spirit, and animal spirits are different from our spirits, and the spirits of angels are also different from ours. And yet, all spirits are basically the same, just as every human is different, but basically every human is the same.

There are also many different types of love. I love my wife, my two sons and all my family. And although I love them all equally, I love them differently. I love my wife with a different love than the love I have for my two sons, and I have a different love for *each* of my two sons, and that's how God's love is. Don't you think that God is capable of having different loves too? He loves all of creation, but each creature receives a different type of love from God. It states all through the Bible that God's creatures worship Him, both on earth and in heaven. In the book of Revelation, it tells us that there are animals in heaven such as cherubims, horses, and other creatures. The verse below plainly states this fact.

"And every creature which is in heaven, and on the earth, and under the earth, and such as are in the sea, and all that are in them, heard I saying, Blessing and honour, and glory and power, be unto him that sitteth upon the throne, and unto the lamb for ever and ever. And the four beasts said, A'-men." (Revelation 5:13-14)

"All the earth shall worship thee, and shall sing unto thee; they shall sing to thy name. Se'-lah."(Psalm 66:4)

Here again we have the animals praising the Lord. In the above verse of Revelation, John the Revelator says that he heard all the creatures speaking praises to God. And in Psalm 66 above, it not only says that the beasts are praising God, but they are *singing* to Him too. You see we humans are not the only creatures that love, know, worship, and sing to God.

"The young lions roar after their prey, and seek their meat from God." (Psalm 104:21)

The animals depend on God for substance just as we do. King Solomon was right when he said that we are on an equal par with beasts, for we all depend on God for everything.

"...Speak unto every fowl, and to every beast of the field. Assemble yourselves, and come; gather yourselves on every side to my sacrifice that I do sacrifice for you, even a great sacrifice upon the mountains of Is'-ra-el, that ye may eat flesh, and drink blood." (Ezekiel 39:17)

"Come and gather yourselves together unto the supper of the great God; That ye may eat the flesh of kings, and the flesh of captains, and the flesh of mighty men, and the flesh of horses, and of them that sit on them, and the flesh of all men, both free and bond, both small and great." (Revelation 19:17-18)

In the two verses above, God is sacrificing *humans* to the animals, by giving the animals *"...the supper of the great God"* just as we will go to the *"Supper of the Lamb"*. As you can see, while we are having our great supper, the animals will be

9

having theirs too. We aren't the only creation that God invites to a holy banquet. (I bet you didn't catch that in the Bible did you? Well don't feel bad, neither did I until Jesus showed me!) Think about it, God is sending a *dinner invitation* to all animals, and not only is He going to sacrifice men to the animals, but God is giving them the most expensive thing on the menu: Kings, Captains, and Mighty men.

> *"And he that sat upon the throne said, Behold*
> *I make all things new. And he said unto me,*
> *Write: for these words are true and faithful."*
> *(Revelation 21:5)*

In the above verse, the Lord says that He will make all things new. And what this means is that, not only will we be made brand new (Glorified bodies), but this also includes animals, plants, and all things on earth. This is the new heaven and earth in the thousand year reign.

> *"The wolf also shall dwell with the lamb, and*
> *the leopard shall lie down with the kid; and the*
> *calf and the young lion and the fatling together;*
> *and a little child shall lead them." (Isaiah 11:6)*

10

Isaiah is also talking about the thousand year reign in the verse above where people and animals will live in harmony. Animals will be there with us and we shall all live together in harmony again and there shall be no fear from harm just like in the Garden of Eden.

> *"And the suckling child shall play on the hole of the asp, and the weaned child shall put his hand on the cockatrice' den. They shall not hurt or destroy in all of my holy mountain: for the earth shall be full of the knowledge of the LORD, as the waters cover the sea." (Isaiah 11:8-9)*

In the above verse, from the book of Isaiah, God is talking about His holy mountain. God is telling us that there will be animals on His holy mountain! And that they will not hurt, nor harm anything, because they will be *full of His knowledge*. Wow, how clear are these words? There will be only love because that is what the knowledge of the Lord is. In the thousand year reign animals will be just like they were in the Garden of Eden when they were plant eaters and Adam and Eve had dominion over them. Adam and Eve had no fear of animals simply because there was no need to fear the beasts of the earth, due to the fact that they were full of the knowledge of the Lord. His power is mighty, and all living creatures will have a *Divine* knowledge given from God.

> *"The beasts of the field shall honour me, the dragons and the owls: because I give waters in the wilderness, and rivers in the desert, to give drink to my people, my chosen." (Isaiah 43:20)*

The verse above shows us again, that all creatures honor and worship God, because His love and mercy are awesome. It also states that He supplies all of us with everything we need; both man and beast alike.

Chapter 3

Learning from Animals

"There be four things which are little upon the earth, but they are exceedingly wise:"
Proverbs 30:24

Part of God's wisdom that He imparts to us is achieved through His animals whether we are aware of it or not. In His word, God *instructs* us to learn from His animals. Let's look at the book of Proverbs which was written by King Solomon, who was the wisest man in history. God gave King Solomon wisdom beyond belief and King Solomon tells us to learn from God's creatures so that we can gain wisdom.

"Go to the ant, thou sluggard; consider her ways, and be wise: Which having no guide, overseer, or ruler, Provideth her meat in the

summer, and gathereth her food in the harvest."
(Proverbs 6:6-8)

Many people believe that animals are dumb, but in the book of Proverbs, God *instructs* us to learn from them. In the verse above King Solomon says to consider the ways of the ant and to be wise like them. Webster's dictionary defines the word *"consider"* as, "To regard with respect or thoughtfulness and to regard with respect or honor; esteem" (Page 285).

In my vision, God instructed me to learn unconditional love, and forgiveness from a dog. He told me that the purpose of sending BJ was to teach me the importance of love and forgiveness.

Although I have heard the importance of love and forgiveness preached in many churches, on many occasions, and in many ways, it took a dog to show me *how* to do it. No man can really show you because men are sinners and they can talk all they want, but talk is cheap. Men will fail you, and I know, because they have all failed me. God tells us not to put our trust in any man but only in Him. A dog does not need to talk; he just does it because a dog's way of communing is by living it. Where I grew up, we had a saying: "Don't talk about it, do it".

And that is exactly what a dog does. Dogs don't talk but you can learn from them by just observing their behavior and traits.

"There be four things which are little upon the earth, but they are exceedingly wise: The ants are a people not strong, yet they prepare their meat in the summer; The conies are but a feeble folk, yet make their houses in the rocks; The locusts have no king, yet go they forth all of them by bands; The spider taketh hold with her hands, and is in kings' palaces." (Proverbs 30:24-28)

In the above verse, God states that His creatures are, "... *exceedingly wise*". How clear is that? God sent me a dog to teach *me* about *Him* and God Himself calls His animals exceedingly wise, so who am I to disagree.

"But ask now the beasts, and they shall teach thee; and the fowls of the air, and they shall tell thee: Or speak to the earth, and it shall teach thee: and the fishes of the sea shall declare unto thee. Who knoweth not in all these that the hand of the LORD hath wrought this? In whose hand

is the soul of every living thing, and the breath
of all mankind." (Job 12:7-10)

The above verse says a mouthful, it tells us to *"ask"* the beasts and fish and they will teach us. Now to ask does not always mean to communicate with the mouth because we can observe and learn from animals and other people. Ask any psychologist and they will tell you that they observe behavior first, because behavior says it all. In psychology there are different modes of learning, but the one I want to point out is called "observational learning". This is when a person or an animal learns from observing another person or animal. A man can watch and learn from an animal or he can watch and learn from another man. And animals can learn from a man or from another animal. A good example would be: Man observed birds which in turn, helped man to build airplanes. When you observe something you are in a way, asking. And so, the Lord is telling us in this verse that if you observe any animal, you can learn from it. The American Indian has known this for years.

It also states that the souls of men and beasts are in God's hand and that His breath is in all of us; man and beast alike. And lastly, the above verse definitely states that animals *do* have spirits because it states, *"the soul of every living thing"*.

16

So there you have it, God is definitely telling us that animals have spirits because he says "every living thing". Can you argue with God? Not me brother.

"Who teacheth us more than the beasts of the earth, and maketh us wiser than the fowls of heaven?" (Job 35:11)

Here in the verse above Job talks of animals teaching us and although it states that God teaches us more than animals, it still says that animals do teach us. The key words here are *"Who teaches us more"* and this implies that animals *do* teach us and if you think about it, God is saying that learning from animals are second only to learning from Him.

Chapter 4

Spirits and God's Love

"God is a Spir'-it: and they that worship him must worship him in spirit and in truth." -John 4:24

In the Bible there are many different "types" of spirits which can be either good or evil because they are either from God or from Satan. The Hebrew meaning of spirit means person, beast, life, and creature. Satan possessed the spirit of a snake in the Garden of Eden and Jesus rebuked men who were possessed by demons or evil spirits.

"For God hath not given us the spirit of fear;
but of power, and of love, and of a sound mind."
(2 Timothy 1:7)

The above verse tells us that there are many different spirits such as the spirits of fear, arrogance, hate, jealousy, sloth, greed, etc. We can see the natural world, but there is also a spirit world because the Bible tells us this. And as a matter of fact, the Bible tells us that *God is a spirit.*

If an evil demon has a spirit then why can't animals? I have never heard of people who died and went to hell and said that they saw their animals there. However, the ones who say that they went to heaven *did* see their pets, or other heavenly animals.

The spirits of animals are *pure truth* but we are not. Have you ever once caught your dog or pet telling you a lie? So the next time someone says that animals don't have spirits please feel free to inform them of these scriptures. It may help them.

"Thou sendest forth thy spirit, they are created: and thou renewest the face of the earth."
(Psalm 104:30)

The verse above shows without a doubt, that animals have spirits because it states that God sends forth His spirit into each living creature; be it human or animal. In Genesis, God breathes His breath of life into all living creatures. If all living things have the breath of God in them, then they have God's spirit; for the breath of God is His spirit.

In the book of Genesis, God instructed Noah to put the animals on the ark in order to save them from the flood. And he also made a covenant with the animals which was the same covenant as the one He made with man.

> *"Of fowls after their kind, and of cattle after their*
> *kind, of every creeping thing of the earth after*
> *his kind, two of every sort shall come unto thee,*
> *to keep them alive." (Genesis 6:20)*

God commanded Noah to keep these creatures alive in order to save them and their seed. The key words in the verse above are *"...to keep them alive"*. This clearly shows that God does not, nor will not destroy all of His animals (Or humans). Not ever. If God wanted to, He would have completely destroyed all the animals during the great flood. Does God destroy animals in the Bible? Yes of course, but He also destroys men and animals alike; but not completely. No matter what anyone may say, He saved animals and men alike on the ark to continue His *entire* creation. Why do people and especially Christians, want to continue to deny that God doesn't care for His creation,

20

nor love them enough to save them and let them live in eternity with Him?

Let's examine how close animals are to God and how much He loves them. Many people just read over the verse below and they fail to see how much God loves all of His creation, simply because people are only interested in His love for them.

> *"Are not two sparrows sold for a farthing? and one of them shall not fall on the ground without your Father." (Matthew 10:29)*

You see, a sparrow does not die without God being there beside him just as He is for us. The verse above tells us that God is there to receive the spirit of that sparrow with open arms at the instant of death. And of course, the verse above is not only showing us how much He loves his animals, but that He loves us even more; *in a different way*. The fact is that when a sparrow dies it falls to the ground. And so therefore, we know from the words in the verse above, that Jesus is talking about the *death* of a bird. He is telling us that even a bird doesn't die without Jesus being right there to take the spirit of that bird to heaven. And if you notice, Jesus says not one will fall without

21

God being there. Which tells us that He is there for every bird, and every creature.

> *"Are not five sparrows sold for two farthings,*
> *and not one of them is forgotten before God?"*
> *(Luke 12:6)*

Here it is stated again for a second time in the above verse. And in this scripture God is telling us that man might not value His sparrows but He certainly does. *"Not one is forgotten."* No... not one.

> *"Consider the ravens: for they neither sow nor*
> *reap;...and God feedeth them: how much more*
> *are ye better than the fowls?" (Luke 12:24)*

In the verse above, Jesus tells us how much God loves us by telling us how much He loves his animals. God is *telling us that he takes care of His animals*. He then tells us that if He takes care of His animals because He loves them, then why wouldn't He do the same for us, because He loves us even more.

*"Who provideth for the raven his food? when his
young ones cry unto God, they wander for lack
of meat." (Job 38:41)*

The young birds cry to God for food because they know that
everything comes from God but sadly, there are many people
who aren't aware of this.

*"Canst thou put an hook into his nose? Or bore
his jaw through with a thorn? Will he make
many supplications unto thee? Will he speak
soft words unto thee? Will he make a covenant with thee? Wilt thou take him for a ser-
vant for ever? Wilt thou play with him as with a
bird? Or wilt thou bind him for they maidens?"
(Job 41:2-5)*

In the above verse, God is talking to Job about one of His
creatures; the Leviathan. This huge and awesome creature gives
prayers and supplications to God and the verse also states that
God plays with him and makes a covenant with this creature.
Notice that God tells Job that this particular beast *"speaks soft
words to God"*.

God is also showing Job how weak men are compared to the Almighty God because God is telling Job that no one but God can create living creatures that have spirits.

God even expects animals to observe the Sabbath (The seventh day) just like he expects man to do. Look at the verse below.

> *"But the seventh day is the Sabbath of the LORD thy God: in it thou shalt not do any work, thou, nor thy son, nor thy daughter, nor thy manservant, nor thy maidservant, nor thine ox, nor thine ass, nor any of thy cattle,..."*
> *(Deuteronomy 5:14)*

God says that no creature, man or beast, is to do any work on the seventh day by issuing the decree that *all* creatures are to rest on the Sabbath day. This scripture plainly shows that the Lord expects animals to observe the Sabbath along with men, and that God has dedicated this day to men and animals alike. Speaking of the seventh day, a dog's age is 7 years to our 1. (7 is God's number.) And if you turn the word dog around, it spells God. I know this is an old saying, but it is true.

Chapter 5

God Preserves the Spirits of Animals

"Thy righteousness is like the great mountains; thy judgments are a great deep: O LORD, thou preservest man and beast." -Psalm 36:6

The word *"preserve"* according to Webster's dictionary means, "To keep alive or in existence, to keep possession of, to make everlasting" (Page 1046). God preserves His animals which can only mean that He takes them to heaven when they die. Where else could they go if God preserves them? Hell is the absence of God and the Bible tells us that there is only heaven or hell. Will our God who is full of love and mercy send innocent animals to hell? Not the God I know, how about yours?

"Thou, even thou, art LORD alone; thou hast made heaven, the heaven of heavens, with all their host, the earth, and all things that are therein, the seas, and all that is therein, and thou preservest them all; and the host of heaven worshippeth thee." (Nehemiah 9:6)

The above verse states without a doubt, that the Lord preserves His creation, and this means all of it. I do not see any exceptions about animals in this verse and God says that He alone preserves *all* of His creation. Look at these words closely, *"...the earth and all things that are therein."* You see, the word therein means *everything*. Or to put it quite simply, all that is in or on the earth.

"Thy righteousness is like the great mountains; thy judgments are a great deep: O LORD, thou preservest man and beast." (Psalm 36:6)

Here the preservation of all spirits is restated again in the verse above. In the Bible, God says that King David was a man after His own heart. The above verse was written by King David and if you read the Bible, you will know how close he was to the Lord. So, if King David says that God preserves *man and beast*, then I believe him; simply because God told him so.

This verse undoubtedly shows that men and animals will be equally preserved and brought to heaven. However men must be saved in order to enter the kingdom of heaven, but animals do not. Hmmm... I guess animals have a one up on us! Here is an analogy to help you understand our equality with animals: although man has dominion over beasts, we are still on an equal par. Although your boss at your job is over you, she or he is still no better than you. (Unless they are not saved, then they are in worst shape than you!)

"For every beast of the forest is mine, and the cattle upon a thousand hills. I know all the fowls of the mountains: and the wild beasts of the field are mine." (Psalm 50:10-11)

Look at the above verse wherein God states that He *knows* all of His animals and that they all know Him. All animals acknowledge God, but in contrast, not all men acknowledge God. And God also says that they are His. God is telling us in this verse that everything is His and He sounds pretty serious about it too because if you notice, the word "mine" is in that small scripture twice.

> *"Who hath prevented me, that I should repay*
> *him? whatsoever is under the whole heaven is*
> *mine." (Job 41:11)*

In the verse above, God tells Job that everything *under* the heaven; which means the earth, belongs to Him.

According to Webster's Dictionary, the word *"whatsoever"* means, "Any or any one of a number of things whether specifically known or not, no matter what; of any kind" (Page 148). And if you notice in the above verse, God uses the word "mine" again.

God states specifically that everything is His. God is telling Job that He created everything and it belongs to Him. And if you read through the verses, you will see that God even asks Job if *he or anyone* can create an animal or a man and put a spirit in them.

> *"A righteous man regardeth the life of his beast:*
> *but the tender mercies of the wicked are cruel."*
> *(Proverbs 12:10)*

28

God tells us in the above verse to treat animals with respect and to be kind to them for they are His. God is also telling us that it is a sin to abuse or hurt them.

Webster's dictionary defines the word *"regard"* as, "To look upon or think of with a particular feeling, to have or show respect or concern for, to think highly of: esteem; to relate to" (Page 1111). You see, God is telling us to love animals.

God regards His creation and tells us do so the same. Please notice that one of the meanings of regard is "to relate to". Let's look at the definition of the word "relate".

Webster's dictionary defines the word *"relate"* as, "To establish an association with, or a connection to" (Page 1114). This shows that God is connected to all of His creation. Which stands to reason that we are all connected to God.

This verse also tells us that only the wicked, or non- believer will treat his or her animals cruelly, because to abuse animals is of Satan. Jesus says you cannot serve two masters, so this verse tells us that if a person mistreats and abuses their animals, they don't know Jesus.

In my vision Jesus told me that He was proud of me and my wife because He knew that we loved animals and that He was also very pleased with the way we treated them. And to think, my wife and I always thought they were *our* animals, simply because we didn't realize that they were a gift from Jesus.

> *"And all flesh shall see the salvation of God."*
> *(Luke 3:6)*

I don't think the verse above really needs too much explanation due to the fact that all flesh means, all creatures. The key word here is, *all*. It states that all creatures or flesh, will see salvation. And isn't salvation required in order to enter into heaven? And the reason for this is because heaven *is* salvation. According to Webster's dictionary *"salvation"* means: "The act of saving from harm or loss; redemption." (Page1164).

Chapter 6

God Blesses His Animals

"And God said unto No'-ah, This is the token
of the covenant, which I have established
between me and all flesh that is upon the earth."
-Genesis 9:17

God did three things for animals *exactly* the same as He did for man. One, God breathed life into animals, the same as He did with man. Two, God blessed animals the same as He did with man. And three, He also made the *same* covenant with animals the same as He did with man. The definition of the word *"bless"* according to Webster's dictionary means, "To sanctify or to make holy. To bestow some benefit upon, or endow with" (Page 142).

So you see God has *bestowed* the benefit of eternal life upon animals and man. However keep in mind, animals can't fall from this endowment of grace, but man can; it's our own choice.

> *"And God blessed them, saying Be fruitful and*
> *multiply..." (Genesis 1:22)*

Now think about those words in the above verse and you can see that God is actually *talking* to the animals by commanding them to procreate. God talks to His animals all through the Bible, which tells us that God talks to animals the same as He does man.

> *"By the word of the LORD, were the heavens*
> *made; and all the host of them by the breath of*
> *his mouth." (Psalm 33:6)*

All creatures were made by, of, and for God, and when He breaths his holy breath He creates life, and that life becomes a part of God; which is eternally connected to God. His word creates the creature and His breath gives the spirit of life.

> *"And I, behold, I establish my covenant with*
> *you, and with your seed after you; and with*

every living creature that is with you,..."
(Genesis 9:9-10)

In the verse above God establishes a covenant with all creatures and their seed which would include the seed of the animals too, and not just men. The proof is in the above verse, where God states, *"...to every living creature."*

"And God said unto No'-ah, This is the token
of the covenant, which I have established
between me and all flesh that is upon the earth."
(Genesis 9:17)

All flesh...this includes animals. God created the rainbow to represent His permanent covenant not just to man, but to all of His creatures. He created the "token" which was the rainbow. This is God's symbol that He has made as an eternal covenant with *both* man and beast. God didn't just put the covenant of the rainbow in the heavens for you; He put it there for your pet too. (Have you ever read the poem "Rainbow Bridge" if not look it up on the internet. It's beautiful).

Chapter 7

God Uses his Animals

"And the LORD God said, It is not good that the man should be alone; I will make him an help meet for him." -Genesis 2:18

In the above verse God uses the words "an help meet" which simply means a companion, teacher, and a helper. God created every animal for a specific purpose. And dogs, cats, and many other creatures were made to be companions to man. They posses God given characteristics such as unconditional love, unconditional forgiveness, and in many instances they also help man.

There are dogs that work along side of fire fighters and dogs that help Police officers, who actually think of their dogs as partners. Dogs herd sheep and in the far north, people utilize dogs for transportation. How many times have we all heard of people who were saved from harm or possible death by their dogs or other animals?

In the book of Jonah, it tells us that a fish saved him so that he in turn, could save thousands of human spirits.

> *"And should not I spare Nin'-e-veh, that great*
> *city, wherein are more than sixscore thousand*
> *persons that cannot discern between their right*
> *hand and their left hand; and also much cattle?"*
> *(Jonah 4:11)*

Of all the books in the Bible, Jonah is my favorite because this guy cracks me up when he tried to run from God. Ha! What was he thinking? The people of Nineveh were sworn enemies of the people of Israel and they were a very evil and sinful people. They killed their enemies and would chop off their heads, then mount the heads on spikes. So you can understand why Jonah didn't want them to receive forgiveness and be saved by the Lord because he thought they deserved to die and go straight to hell.

Jonah had the spirits of hate, fear, and unforgiveness in his heart. Yet God still used Jonah to perform the biggest revival ever known to man in all of human history. And "a great fish" helped to accomplish this awesome feat. (And still, he was mad with God because he thought that God was too merciful and forgiving. This definitely gives us a keen insight into the character of God and His long suffering patience and love.)

"Now the LORD had prepared a great fish to swallow up Jo'-nah. And Jo'-nah was in the belly of the fish three days and three nights." *(Jonah 1: 17)*

In the book of Jonah the scriptures tell us that Jonah spent three days in the belly of the fish and was then spit out by the great fish. This was a "type" of burial and resurrection which symbolized the burial and resurrection of our Lord Jesus. And when Jesus had risen from the dead he delivered our redemption and salvation to us, which parallels the story of Jonah being spit from the mouth of the whale, making Jonah a type of savior for the people of Nineveh.

If the fish had not saved Jonah, then he would not have been able to save all those lost spirits that were in Nineveh. So you see, technically the fish *saved* those people because if the fish had not *saved* Jonah, then Jonah could not have possibly *saved* all those lost spirits in the great city of Nineveh.

The fish that God sent to save Jonah was responsible for saving thousands of human souls (including Jonah). Think about that for a moment, I have *never* saved thousands of souls, but *a fish* has! So basically a fish that many people claim has no spirit, converted more people to God than I ever have, or for that matter, anyone else that I have ever known. Hmmm... God is awesome and so are His animals.

According to God, those who don't believe in Him are fools, because He states that the people who lived in Nineveh couldn't tell their right hand from their left! (They were fools, unbelievers, and lost spirits). And God even asked Jonah, what about all that cattle? Because God didn't want to kill all the animals due to the sins of humans. God was actually telling Jonah that He wanted to save the animals too. Because to God, they were just as important as the people of Nineveh; or he would not even have mentioned the cattle at all. The King of Nineveh tells all the people *and the beasts* to repent. He says,

> "...*Let neither man nor beast, herd nor flock,*
> *taste anything: let them not feed, nor drink water.*
> *But let man and beast be covered with sackcloth,*
> *and cry mightily unto God:...*" *(Jonah 3:7-8)*

The king commands that all the creatures, man and beast alike cry mightily unto the Lord in order to repent and save their lives. (And can you believe it, Jonah actually went outside the city and made a booth to sit in so that he could watch and cheer when God destroyed the people of Nineveh. He didn't know much about forgiveness, did he? And this guy was a priest! Maybe he should have owned a dog).

Balaam's jackass talked to him in the book of Numbers. Jesus allowed the jackass to see the Angel of the Lord before he let Balaam see it. And the jackass *saved* Balaam's life, for the Lord was angry at Balaam. The spirit of greed was in him, for Balaam was a very greedy man, and he went against the desires of God.

Now the Angel of the Lord was barring the way and only the jackass could see Him. Three times Balaam rebuked (Hit) his jackass for stopping and trying to get off the trail, and finally the Angel of the Lord allowed Balaam to see him too.

> *"Then the LORD opened the eyes of Ba'- laam,*
> *and he saw the angel of the LORD standing in*
> *the way,..." (Numbers 22:31)*

And then the Angel rebukes Balaam saying,

"...Wherefore hast thou smitten thine ass these three times? behold, I went out to withstand thee, because thy way is perverse before me. And the ass saw me, and turned from me these three times: unless she had turned from me, surely now also I had slain thee, and saved her alive." (Numbers 22:32-33)

This verse clearly shows that God gave more reverence to the jackass than He did to Balaam; a human. The angel says he would have shown mercy to the animal, but not to Balaam. In other words, the angel claims that he would have killed Balaam and spared the animal. He was a real rascal, that one! He actually thought he could hide his spirits of lust and greed from the Lord. And of course when Balaam saw the angel, he bowed proclaiming that he was a sinner, and crying out his repentance. But as you can see, the animal saw the angel *first*, and she bowed *first* in worship, knowing it was Jesus. *The jackass knew it was Jesus.*

And it's quite obvious that the angel didn't like the fact that Balaam had hit the animal three times, because if you notice, this is the *first* question that he asks Balaam. The angel asks, why are you abusing my creature?

So if you really study the verse above, you will see that between Balaam and the jackass, the jackass was the smartest. And the jackass saw the angel first, due to his sinless nature.

"And when the ass saw the angel of the LORD, she
fell down under Ba'Laam:..." (Numbers 22:27)

The jackass actually bowed when she saw Jesus because she knew instantly who it was. I believe that the above scripture clearly shows that the Angel of the Lord was Jesus, before he came to earth in human form, due to the fact that the angel said, "...*because your ways are perverse to me*". Only the Lord reserves the right to say that. That is a judgment, and only Jesus has the authority to judge. You can learn a lot from a jackass. So the next time someone calls you that, bless them.

Now let's examine the book of Kings. Let's see how God uses His birds to help Elijah. (He was like the superman of the Old Testament. He out ran a horse drawn chariot!)

"And it shall be, that thou shalt drink of the
brook; and I have commanded the ravens to
feed thee there...And the ravens brought him
bread and flesh in the morning, And bread and

flesh in the evening; and he drank of the brook."
(1 Kings 17:4-6)

God commanded the birds to feed Elijah by the brook Cherith. The ravens not only brought him bread to eat, but also flesh. (Flesh is another word in the Bible that speaks of all creatures, both man and beast).

Here we have another example of how the Lord uses His animals to help humans, and of course this is a different animal which shows that the Lord uses many different types of animals in order to achieve His plans. In this story God uses His creatures to help Elijah stay alive in the wilderness.

"And it came to pass, as they still went on, and talked, that, behold, there appeared a chariot of fire, and horses of fire, and parted them both asunder; and E-li'-jah went up by a whirlwind into heaven." (2 Kings 2:11)

While Elisha and Elijah were walking along the Jordan River a "chariot of fire" pulled by "horses of fire" appeared and a whirlwind took Elijah to heaven; while he was still *alive*. The prophet Elijah was the superman of the Old Testament

41

and he was one of two prophets that never died in this world (the other was Enoch) and he had two awesome encounters with God's creatures. Elijah was such a great man of God that God honored Elijah by sending more than one creature to help him. God sent him a *flock* of creatures to keep him alive, and He sent a *herd* of creatures to escort him to heaven; while he was still alive.

Jonah was only blessed with *one beast* to help him and Balaam was only blessed with *one beast* to help him, but Elijha was blessed with many.

God had such regard for Elijah that he honored him by sending two groups of animals, from two different species, in order to bless him. Now think about it, if a bird fed you and kept you alive for months, and horses that were on fire came to take you to heaven, knowing that you did not have to suffer the pangs of death, would you think that you had been blessed? And God Almighty did this with His animals because *He commanded it to be so*.

In the book of Acts, God uses many species of animals to tell the Apostle Peter that the Gentiles were no longer unclean, due to the blood of Christ on the cross. And at that time in history, Jewish people were not allowed to even touch a Gentile, let alone enter their house. In his vision, this is what Peter saw and heard,

> "...*heaven opened, and a certain vessel descending unto him, as it had been a great sheet knit at the four corners, and let down to earth: Wherein were all manner of four-footed beasts of the earth, and wild beasts, and creeping things, and fowls of the air.*" *(Acts 10: 11-12).*

The verse above describes the manner in which God gave Peter this awesome message. God compares the Jewish people to the Gentiles, using clean and unclean animals. God told Peter to kill and eat, and Peter told God that he didn't eat unclean animals, and God said,

> "...*What God hath cleansed, that call not thou common. This was done thrice: and the vessel was received up again into heaven*". *(Acts 10:15-16)*

In the above verse, God tells Peter that He had cleansed all men with the blood of Christ. As you can see, God used his animals to send Peter an awesome message; that *now*, all people including Gentiles, could be baptized and saved. But read carefully and you will notice that the animals *came from heaven and went back to heaven*. It states that the animals were "received into heaven again". And look at all the animals he used. I guess that awesome message took a lot of animals to deliver, and they were all from heaven. And then they went back to heaven.

God then sent Peter to the house of a Gentile named Cornelius where God commanded Peter to baptize Cornelius and his family in the Holy Spirit. And after the spirit fell on them all, Peter said,

> *"...Of a truth I perceive that God is no respecter of persons: But in every nation he that feareth him, and worketh righteousness, is accepted with him". (Acts 10:34-35)*

The message that was brought to Peter through the use of these heavenly animals, is what is commonly referred to as, "the good news". And animals helped to deliver this awesome news.

Let's move on and examine the book of Joel and the visions that he had of the end times as a prophet of God. Below Joel is talking about God's army in the battle of Armageddon where we the saints, assist Jesus when he finally brings righteousness and judgment to a corrupt earth.

> *"The appearance of them is as the appearance*
> *of horses; and as horsemen, so shall they run."*
> *(Joel 2:4)*

Did you know that all the saints will be fighting along side Jesus in the end of the age? We saints will be what is Biblically known as, "Joel's Army". And we will be riding what "appear" to be horses, and notice that it says *"appears to be"*. The reason for this is because they are not earthly horses; they are spirit horses that resemble the ones on earth so that they "appear" as horses. These horses are from heaven and sent by God, and the verse above describes how we will look and what we will be riding on; spirit horses of fire (Just like Elijha).

The scripture tells us that the children of God (The saints or all saved people) will be part of the army along with our heavenly animals. Oh, and Jesus will be riding His white horse!

I pray that I get to ride on BJ and we can defeat death together.

PART II

"How long wilt thou forget me,
O LORD? For ever? How long
wilt thou hide thy face from me?

-Psalm 13:1

Chapter 8

Meeting And Adopting BJ

"And all flesh shall see the salvation of God."
-Luke 3:6

If your family is like mine, then I know that you think of your pets as children, because after all they are part of the family.

I have owned three dogs in my life and all three dogs were special to me however one stood out from the rest, and his name was BJ. At first I thought it was because I was getting old and more sentimental, or maybe it was because I knew that he had been very badly abused. But I was to find out much later it was because he was anointed and sent by God.

BJ was a gray and white Shih Tzu and he came to us by surprise. My son lived in a development and he saw his neighbors abusing BJ. The owners had BJ tied outside on a short chain with two other dogs that were bigger than he was. BJ was chained there night and day and he had to compete for food with the other two dogs. As you can imagine, he didn't get very much to eat. When BJ lived with us he would take a piece of dog food out of his bowl and go hide under the table to eat it because he was afraid that Petie our other dog, or one of us would take his food from him. He did this up to the day he passed even after Petie was gone. And many times they would take the other dogs inside, but they would leave BJ outside because they said he was bad. And BJ stayed outside, even when it was storming; all by himself.

It hurt my son to see BJ being treated this way. So one day my son told the owners, "You have two choices; give me the dog, or I'm calling the police and report you for animal abuse, because I can't watch that dog suffer any longer". And so they handed the dog over to him.

The woman who owned BJ told my son that BJ had been to several homes but it had never worked out, claiming that he was too dangerous because he bit everyone who got near him. (If someone treated me like that, I think that I would probably bite them too). She said the dog was no good and that her husband was thinking about shooting him anyway because they had decided that he was worthless. So the woman gave BJ to my son right then and there.

I remember when I first saw BJ at my son's house I asked him, "What in the world is that?" BJ was just standing there staring at me and you could barely see his eyes due to the long fur on his face. There were flea bites all over him and he had a flea nest full of eggs on his back. His hair was missing in many spots and had been replaced by red bloody bite marks from his teeth where he had been biting and chewing in order to get relief from what must have been an excruciating and burning pain from all the flea bites. And at that time I didn't know that he had never received any love, attention, or companionship and that he was scared of lightening.

Not long after my son took ownership of the dog he had to move and so he informed us that the landlord of the new apartment where he was moving did not allow dogs, and he wanted to know if we would take him. We all agreed that if he took him to the dog pound, no one would take BJ due to his horrible condition and age. We knew that they would more than likely put him to sleep, so my wife and I agreed to adopt him.

When my son brought BJ over to my house he didn't look as bad as he had when I first saw him. My son had clipped and cleaned him the best he could, considering the fact that BJ was quick to bite and he had a very nasty bite. My son had cut the flea nest off and as much of the knotted hair as he possibly could. Now I could see his eyes and he was able to walk better. But he still smelled bad because my son did not dare to try and wash him and you could tell that the only bath he had had in years was God's rain.

My son informed me that two of BJ's ribs had knots where he had been kicked and the bones had been broken and left to mend on their own, and the foul odor was due to an untreated and neglected skin rash.

At that time we already had a dog named Petie but we decided to take BJ in and give him a home in order to save his life. Petie would just have to adjust to the new member of the family. Petie wasn't too happy at first about the new situation, but we knew our house was the last stop before death for this poor dog. Petie was a Boston terrier and he had been with us since he was a little puppy and he had been king of the house for eight years. At first we did have some problems with Petie because he was jealous of BJ, but eventually it worked out.

My wife and I tried to clean him up and clip his hair some more. We managed to cut some of the hair knots from around his feet and legs but he kept trying to bite us. My wife and I finally came up with a brilliant idea and we bought some flea and anti-biotic spray. We tried spraying BJ with medicine, but he would run from us. We could only get a small amount of the spray on him, but it did seem to help somewhat. But after a while, he would run and hide as soon as he would see the spray bottle. He wasn't dumb!

We took BJ to the Veterinarian and got all his shots and they estimated his age at about eight years old. He got all his shots and he seemed to be doing a little better however, we still weren't able to cut his hair the way it should be cut without getting bit. So we came to the conclusion that we needed a professional and finally we got wise and took him to a dog groomer. Long story made short, we took him to the dog groomers and continued to spray him when possible and after several months of loving care BJ became the traditional caterpillar that turned into a beautiful butterfly. He became the cutest thing you ever saw. His bloody spots and skin rash went away, his hair was cut nicely, and he got a bath on a regular basis.

He had a mournful, sad expression, but you could see some gratefulness in his big black round eyes and he was so quiet that sometimes you forgot he was even there. He slowly began to get used to his surroundings but we still couldn't touch or pet him. And to think of holding him close was just out of the question. As I stated, a woman and her two young daughters had abused him badly and apparently the children had been taught by their mother that abusing animals was just fine. BJ was afraid of females more than males. He had a bad case of PTSD which stands for Post Traumatic Stress Disorder. This disorder is mainly associated with veterans of a war era who have seen battle however it can affect people (and animals) in other devastating experiences such as, child and *animal* abuse, child molestation, deaths, car wrecks, parents divorcing, etc.

My son told me that one time he and his girlfriend left BJ at her dad's house while they went away to a movie, and upon their return they didn't see BJ anywhere. When she asked her dad where BJ was, he said the dog had slipped out and gotten lost. Not one person in the house had tried to look for BJ and it was beginning to storm as my son and his girlfriend got in their car and began to search for BJ. They drove everywhere looking for him and finally after an hour long search they finally found him huddled under a big tree, soaking wet and shaking uncontrollably, from the thunder and lightening. When I heard that story it just about tore my heart out. God had saved BJ.

After we had BJ for about a month my wife's mother asked if she could take BJ and at this point, I still didn't think BJ should be with us because of Petie, but I had my doubts about giving the dog to her too. She said she wanted him due to the fact that she lived alone and she wanted the dog for company when we weren't there. I thought that BJ had made some progress and maybe it would work out. So my wife and I decided to give her the dog and the great thing about it was that we would be able to see BJ whenever we wanted. And the fact was that we really couldn't deal with two dogs anyway, especially the way Petie was acting. So this seemed to be the best solution and we could still see BJ.

We informed her of his abusive past and told her to be very careful with him. We told her that she had to go slow with him for a week or two until he got used to her and we warned her not to try and pet him or give him a bath right away. Two days later my mother-in-law called us on the phone crying. She said that the dog had bit her and she asked us if we would take him back. God bless her heart. God didn't want her to have this special dog because he wasn't meant for her; he was meant for me, which I later came to realize.

We went over to her house and got BJ and we took him back home with us. About a week later her house burned down. Luckily she got out without any harm however, I sincerely believe that if BJ had been there he would have hid under the bed from fear, and would have more than likely burned up in the fire. He had escaped death from his abusers, getting lost, getting shot, and taken to the pound to be exterminated, and now, a deadly house fire.

When my son learned about the fire he shared several sto-ries about BJ with me and my wife. He told us that he and his girlfriend had taken BJ on some of their camping trips because BJ loved to go camping. He told us that they would float down the creek on these trips and BJ would go with them. They bought a little baby blow up boat and BJ would float right along with them. They tied BJ's boat to their inner tubes and they would all float down the creek together; they on their inner tubes and BJ in his little boat. I learned that BJ had been a sailor just like me!

And he said that on one of their trips, he and his friends were sitting by the fire and it was night, when he noticed move-ment up on the hill, and when he looked up he saw two glowing green eyes and he knew it was a bobcat. The big cat then came straight down to their fire and they had to grab BJ and run to the safety of their cars. My son said that he believed that the big cat wanted to make BJ into a meal. He said that they all had to sit in their cars until morning because the cat refused to leave. The cat had no fear of them and had walked into the campsite and lay down by the fire! All their camping gear and food was by the campsite and out of reach. The big cat decided to stay by the fire and did not leave until the morning daylight. This happened at a lake deep in the woods and I believe that it was a momma cat looking to feed her young.

BJ had escaped another date with death. He escaped being abused, being shot, being taken to the pound, being exterminated, being burned up in a house fire, and being eaten. BJ and I were bound together by God and little did I or BJ know, that God was at work. God had a plan; a rendezvous between a human spirit and an animal spirit. Two different spirits were to meet in order to teach us both about love and forgiveness and to give me a greater understanding of how much the Lord loves His handiwork.

We had BJ for six great years and then he died.

Chapter 9

Getting to Know BJ

"Are not five sparrows sold for two farthings,
and not one of them is forgotten before God?"
-Luke 12:6

O ver the first year we had taken BJ in he managed to bite us quite a few times. And the first six months he was here, he stayed in our computer room and would rarely come out except to eat or go out (believe it or not he was house trained). Many times my wife and I would have to pick him up and carry him outside so he could do his business. He would rarely come out of the room and when he did, he would just stand at the end of the hall and stare at us. We would literally have to go pick him up and take him out. We knew he was scared, and that we were taking a chance on getting bit, but we had to do it. And on several occasions he did try to bite whoever it was that was brave enough to carry him outside which was usually me. We basically had to carry him at arm's length while holding him in the middle of his little body so he couldn't bite us.

On days that I was at work, my wife had to take him out to use the bathroom. This went on for several weeks but then one day my wife tried to pick him up and he bit her. Although it was not a bad bite, she was afraid to pick him up after that, so she tried to coax him inside but he just stood at the end of the driveway and stared at her. We believed that in his mind he thought that he was not allowed in the house, or perhaps he was used to being outside, or maybe he just wanted to stay away from possible abuse. But we knew he didn't like females.

She called my son to come by the house and carry BJ inside. My son has a job where he is on the road a lot so he could stop by and help with the dog. BJ trusted my son up to a point. He would allow my son to pick him up without biting him but if he tried to give him a bath or cut his hair, BJ would bite him. This was only because BJ had lived with my son for several months and he and BJ had grown somewhat close to each other. So this was the new routine when I was at work. My wife would let BJ out and if he would not come back inside, she called my son and he would come by the house and put BJ back inside.

Over the first few weeks we talked to BJ and gave him treats, and quite often my wife and I would even sing to him, trying to win his trust. Eventually his favorite song became "Somewhere over the Rainbow" and Petie's favorite song was "When you Wish Upon a Star".

Eventually I coaxed him up on the bed and he began to get used to being on the bed at night while I watched television. But one night as I was lying in bed, I decided to pet his head and he decided to bite my hand. And he really got me good. I was rubbing around his ears and I guess I just got too close to his mouth and it must have scared him, because all of a sudden he bit me and when he bit me, he held on and just kept chewing. My immediate reaction of course was to let out a loud yell which made him finally let go of my finger. I ran to the sink and washed my hand and then cleansed the bite with alcohol. I put pressure on the wound until it finally stopped bleeding and then I bandaged it and thought it would be ok. Two days later my hand had become so swollen that I had no choice but to go to the hospital and get medical treatment. The doctor had to re-open the wound and flush it. She scolded me for waiting two days before coming to get help but I didn't mind, because I was more worried that someone would ask me questions about what had happened. And of course, I knew that they would recognize a dog bite. And when this happens the doctor will ask you about the dog's shot history. And then there was the possibility that they would consider putting the dog down if they felt it was a danger to other people. But the doctor did not ask me anything at all, and I thought that I could leave with no questions asked, and BJ would be safe. So I went to the front desk to get my antibiotics for the infection thinking that I would be happily on my way. But when I got to the front desk the nurse informed me that the animal control man wanted to talk with me and that was exactly what my wife and I had feared. They had called the Animal Control office to report a dog bite which is now a law, and of course it was one that they had to follow. The animal control man began to ask questions about my dog and he made mention about taking BJ to the pound. So I did some fast talking and said some prayers to myself. He asked me if BJ had ever bitten anyone else before and I told him no, this was the first time he had ever bitten anyone. Yes, I told a lie but I did repent afterwards and yes of course BJ had bitten someone, he had bitten everyone in the family except the grandchildren, including my mother-in-law, but this guy didn't need to know that. He then asked if BJ had all of his shots and I told him that he had received all of his shots not more than a few months ago. He looked at me with a serious look and asked me if I thought the dog would be a danger to anyone else and I told him no. I explained to him that it was my fault for getting to close to his mouth. And finally he wanted to know if there were any small children at home that would be in danger of getting bit. I informed him that my grandchildren came over to visit often, but we never allowed them to get near, or pet the dog. I explained a little about BJ's past abuse and told him that the dog was getting much better and that if he took BJ to the pound they would only have to kill him because no one would want him.

Finally, he said that I could take him back home but only on several conditions. Number one, if they got a report of this same dog biting anyone else again they would dispose of him. And two, BJ and I were to be placed on a one week parole and the conditions of parole were that I had to keep him on a leash, and he was not allowed off my property. And lastly, I had to call the animal control office every day to update him on the status of BJ's behavior. The animal control man told me that he was assigned to BJ's case and that I had to call and ask for him by name.

BJ had been assigned an animal case worker and both of us had been placed on parole. We were now two of America's most wanted and BJ had escaped yet another death sentence with the help of Jesus. Praise God! I tried to make a joke and I asked the animal control man if they needed to take a mug shot of me and BJ together. But he didn't think that was very funny. I ignored BJ for two or three days after he bit me. I did not speak to him, except to tell him that he was a "bad dog" while showing him my finger. He would put his head down in shame and I could tell this upset him very much. I think that he realized that I truly loved him, and that he may have lost the one person in his abused life that actually loved him. BJ could not understand why I didn't hit him because this was not the usual reaction from humans that he was used to. After all, everyone else had hit him, why not this human too? After a few days of ignoring him I just knew in my heart that he would never bite me again, however at the time I didn't know that it was God telling me. Sure enough, after that incident we began to grow closer day by day. So now armed with a new confidence, a little courage, and a little faith that he would not bite me, I began to via for his affection. I vowed that one day I would hug and kiss him.

We gradually became inseparable and everyone in the family and all our friends that knew BJ, were amazed at the change. But still no one else in the family could pick him up and pet him. My son's girlfriend referred to him as "Beast J".

After a long period of time he would allow my wife to pet him, but only when he wanted it. He would walk over to my wife sometimes, which was his way of saying you have my permission to pet me, and he would allow her to pet him. But when he walked away, it was hands off.

Eventually it got to the point where I could pick him up and kiss his face and he would lie back in my arms like a baby. Sometimes I would hold him up on my chest while I stood, and he would put his chin on my shoulder and look over the top of my shoulder. Then as time progressed he began to lick me at night before going to bed and would sleep beside me. I was getting kisses from BJ! And he would always stare at me as if to say, "You love me? Why? Why don't you hit me, all the other humans do?"

I just knew in my heart that he had no intentions of ever biting me again. I could see the love for me in his eyes. In his eyes was the look of one who seeks forgiveness, trust, and love. He had figured out that I was different from anyone else he had known, and he was beginning to enjoy being pampered. I had forgiven him for biting me, and he had forgiven humans for abusing him. And I know that if I had hit him that night long ago, we would never have bonded.

BJ turned out to be a wonderful companion and the last two years were the best, because BJ and I had become best buddies. We spent many hours together until he passed. We spent many nights out back on our deck by the campfire. He actually began to show his little personality those last two years, rather than being in the survival mode. When I came home in the evening, BJ would get one of his toys and begin to play, rolling around on his back and tossing the toy in the air. He was happy that I was home. My wife said he would mope around all day until about 10:30pm. Then he would wander out of his room, walk down the hall and sit on the rug at the back door, waiting for me to come home from work. He knew I got home around 11pm. BJ could tell time! Finally for once in his life he could be a dog; a dog that was loved and cared for.

BJ died on October 18, 2011, the day before my wife's birthday and I cannot describe how crushed I was. This made me draw much closer to Jesus. I needed solace and relief from the pain because he was like a child to me. I have never had such an intense love for any of my other dogs and I grew up with one as a child. His name was Duke and he was a hound dog. So I cried and I prayed, and I demanded that Jesus let me see him one more time; just once. I needed to know where he was and if he was he ok. I needed to know if he was free of pain, or if he even existed anymore. I had a burning need to know if he went to heaven with Jesus or did he just die, and that was the end of him. I HAD TO KNOW! So I took it to Jesus and I quoted His own words back to him. Jesus tells us to ask and we shall receive. So I asked... many times.

Chapter 10

The First Vision

"Give ear to my words, O Lord, consider my meditation." -Psalm 5:1

About two months before his passing BJ began to show signs of weakness. His hearing and his eyesight began to fail and he began to lose his coordination. Our back porch is just a one step block of cement and several times when BJ tried to hop up onto the porch, he missed and bumped his chin.

The last nine days prior to his passing, it was really noticeable that he was beginning to decline rapidly. On many occasions when BJ had to go out to do his business, my wife and I actually had to take him out and hold him up because he unable to stand on his own. Then there would be several hours off and on through the day where he seemed like he was going be to be fine.

I woke up Sunday morning and saw that BJ's left eye was bleeding and although it was a small amount, it scared me. The only animal hospital that was open happened to be in another state which was a little over an hour and a half away. I had no other choice but to drive there. I will never forget that day, it was a beautiful warm autumn day and the wind was blowing very hard. So I wrapped BJ up in his favorite little blanket and off we went.

When we arrived at the hospital we had to wait for about thirty minutes and I was beginning to become impatient, and not to mention I was somewhat scared. A young lady and her dog were next in line ahead of us and when she saw the condition of BJ, she told the nurse to take my dog first. She said that her dog had eaten a tennis ball and it wasn't an emergency. She could see how bad BJ looked. (God bless her wherever she is). As a matter of fact, there were five other people there with their pets and they were all staring at BJ; he looked that bad. I knew they were all thinking, "That poor guy, his dog is almost dead and he refuses to see it. I'd sure hate to be the one who has to tell him. I feel bad for that poor nurse, because she has to be the one to tell him".

A few minuets later the doctor came out and they took BJ into the clinic and they were gone for about twenty-five minutes. When they came out they gave BJ back to me and the nurse asked me if I would step outside so that we could talk. I thought to myself, this is not a good sign. She then told me that she was sure that he was suffering from renal failure and she told me she was going to give BJ four different medicines and see what happens. One of which they had to draw blood from BJ and mix his blood with the medicine. She told me this one was for his eyes. I told the nurse that there had been mucus forming on his eyelids for several days, matting his eyes shut so that he couldn't open them. For several days my wife and I had to take a warm wash cloth and put on his eyes in order to get the gook out of his eyes so that he could open them. The nurse told me that the eye drops would help that problem and also help with the infection.

After we got the medicines BJ and I left. We stopped at a fast food place and got a cheeseburger for me, and small fries for BJ. He loved fries and he ate them with no problem. This gave me some hope because I thought that an appetite was a good sign of recovery.

I prayed and begged Jesus to let him live a little longer. I begged Him to please let me have another week at least, so I could pay constant attention to him. I began to have those regrets where you beat yourself up for not paying more attention to your loved one before they become sick or died. Then you start to beat yourself up telling yourself that you should have spent more time with them. If only I had known that BJ might die this day I would go back and change things. If only I could do it over again I would do it all differently. Good old hind site! Yet you know in your heart that in the real world, living life takes time away from things you love. You realize that you can't spend every second of your day and night with the ones you love, but you can be more loving when you are around them. I knew this but Jesus made me really think hard about it, and when you realize something and really think hard about it, you began to change.

That night I put BJ in his little bed by ours. It was about 11:30pm and my wife had already gone to bed and so I decided to take a bath before giving BJ his medicine. I decided to pray first so I got on my knees in the bathroom and I prayed and cried to Jesus to please let my dog live, if only a while longer. And in an instant Jesus came to me in a vision.

In most of the visions I have had, everything around me falls away and Jesus takes me somewhere else. The room fell away instantly and I was in some part of heaven. I have had several visions prior to this one and Jesus had told me that two of the places He had taken me before were what He called my "mansions". However, this place was the same place that I had gone to in my first vision when I was at church, a month after I had been saved. I was out in space and it was dark but I could see. There were stars all around me, but they were strangely shaped and my pastor told me they were angels. They were very bright, but I could look right at them without hurting my eyes. As a matter of fact, when I looked at them they made me feel peaceful and safe. It was extremely quiet, like being in a vacuum. It was only Jesus and me. We were suspended in space just floating but we weren't moving. My body had no weight and I could only see in front of me and to the right and to the left. Jesus was about fifteen feet away when I saw Him and He was wearing a white robe and his whole being glowed with a bright light, but it wasn't a blinding light it was a calming light. Jesus was radiant and beautiful (I generally don't call men beautiful) and His head was tilted to one side just looking at me like I was unique. I could feel His love all over my being and His voice was soft but strong. I was staring at Him and He was smiling at me with His lips closed. It was a knowing smile that you see when you look into someone's eyes and realize that they know something you don't. His eyes were smiling too and they shone as though they were wet like they were sparkling. He spoke to me without moving his lips and I could hear Him in my mind and I know this because He never stopped smiling nor did He open his lips. It seemed as though His mind was my mind, like we were one. Jesus said, *"I have to take BJ home now. It's time for him to come back to me. I will take him late in the morning. I love BJ and I miss him too. He is mine. Everything that I have created belongs to me, and everything that I have created comes back to me. BJ was a gift to you just as everything in this world is a gift. I know that you and your wife love animals and you have done very well taking care of my creature. But his time is over. He found your love, and you found mine. I will give you until late morning to say good-bye then I will take him home."*

Jesus' expression and His eyes were very kind and loving as though He was proud and very pleased with me. He had no qualms about taking BJ and Jesus wanted to make sure I understood that BJ was His, and only on loan to me as a gift. I suddenly realized that I did not create BJ, and I truly had no claim on him. The instant He spoke those last words the vision was gone and I was back in my bathroom. I felt as though Jesus had just left me hanging. And true to His word, He took my dog late the next morning at 10:15 am. I went into the bedroom and picked BJ up and put him in the middle of our bed. I wanted him close to me. I forgot about taking a bath because I didn't care about anything except being close to BJ.

I was so sad and depressed I didn't even bother to give BJ his medicine because I knew it was no use. I knew that Jesus had spoken to me and that He would take BJ in the morning. Besides, at that point in time I would have had to jam the medicine in his mouth because he would not take it or swallow it. BJ just lay there in the bed looking at me. When I got into bed my wife sleepily asked me if I had given BJ his medicine and I said no. I was crying but I didn't want her to know. And I didn't tell her what Jesus had told me, because I knew it would upset her. I knew BJ would be leaving in the morning to be with Jesus because there was no doubt in my mind, that my vision was real. I stayed awake as long as possible so that I could pet him and talk to him, but sometime during the night I fell asleep.

He died late in the morning at 10:15am, just like Jesus said. It was October 18, 2011, one day before my wife's birthday. I was mad at Jesus when BJ died and I threw a fit. I told the Lord I was done with Him because He didn't allow BJ to live and He didn't honor my prayers. I felt that Jesus had come to tell me that He was taking my best friend from me, and then He just left me. An hour later I buried BJ under the apple tree beside Petie and when I was done, I threw another fit. How could Jesus do this to me, how cruel! After about an hour I calmed down from my temper tantrum and I prayed and asked for forgiveness. Jesus answered me and said, *"You are forgiven Steven. Even I dropped the cross at Calvary and a man had to help me to pick it up to complete my journey. Pick up your cross and continue to follow me. I will never leave you. And if you drop the cross like I did, just pick it back up again and continue your journey. There are only two choices, pick the cross up or walk over it. But if you walk over it, you walk away from me."*

I was back in His grace but I was still mad, but not at Jesus. I was mad at death. I hated death and I realized that Satan and man had brought death into this world. I then understood the words in the Gospel where Jesus tells us that Satan is a murderer. I hated Satan and I hated death, but I still wanted to know why Jesus didn't answer my prayers and let BJ live. I was not giving up. And I was also determined to see BJ one last time, if he still existed.

When Jesus told me about the man Simen, (Who happened to be passing by, and was made to help Jesus pick up the cross, and help carry it up the hill.) *(Mark 15:21)* I knew Jesus was telling me that I needed to call another Christian and talk. He knew I needed help to take up my cross, in order to finish my journey. Somehow I had to put my sorrow behind me and find out why my prayers had not been answered. And I just had to know the answer to the question that was burning inside me; "Why did you take my BJ from me?"

Chapter 11

The Second Vision

"O LORD, thou hast searched me, and known me." -Psalm 139:1

After BJ's death I prayed for three weeks asking Jesus to let me see BJ one more time. I needed to see BJ and find out if he was with Jesus, or if he was just a pile of dust. But I got no answer from Jesus. Nothing. I was beginning to think that Jesus had abandoned me, or maybe I had made him mad and He was done with me. Then one evening while I was relaxing in my easy chair and praying to Jesus, begging Him to please let me see BJ just one more time. If only just to see his little face and tell him I loved him. But Jesus still would not answer me, so I began to pray the thirteenth Psalm: *"How long wilt thou forget me, O LORD? for ever? how long wilt thou hide thy face from me? How long shall I take counsel in my soul, having sorrow in my heart daily? how long shall mine enemy be exalted over me?"* (Psalm 13:1-2) I had my eyes closed praying. I just kept praying it over and over and finally I just gave up and sat there and cried.

All of a sudden the whole room fell away and I saw the most amazing thing. I was in a huge beautiful field and I could only see a peripheral view of the field. I was able to see in front of me, to the left and to the right, but I couldn't turn around to see behind me. The field was absolutely beautiful and I noticed that the grass was a vivid green and there were flowers of all colors; colors that I have never seen before. I knew I was in some part of heaven but I didn't know where. The sky was perfectly clear and blue and I could see a huge purple mountain in the distance. And I noticed that there was a tree line at the bottom of the mountain. The trees looked as though they were moving but I felt no wind. As I looked around I could see beautiful butterflies flying in the air all around me. I saw birds and other animals in the distance but I couldn't distinguish what kind they were because they were too far away. I saw small things floating, flying, and jumping in the air, like you would see after hay has been cut. I believe some were seed-spores and some were small insects but I can't really say for sure.

The air was clean and refreshing and I smelled something sweet and pleasant which seemed to put me at ease, and made my whole body seem invigorated. It must have been the flowers that I smelled. And when I looked at them, they seemed alive. And then I saw Jesus walking towards me and there were three dogs following Him and they were jumping all around Him. But they were still a good distance from me, but as they came closer, excitement ran through me because I realized that one of the dogs was BJ! And as I continued to look I realized that one of the other dogs was Petie! But the third one I didn't recognize. And then for a moment I was completely stunned, because I realized that the third dog was my childhood dog and companion, Duke.

Jesus was walking with His arms bent at the elbows with His palms out and the dogs were playing, running, and jumping around Him. They were jumping up and licking His hand and their full attention was on Jesus as though they were all competing for His attention. All three dogs were young, full of energy, and absolutely beautiful. They had a glow that radiated from their young strong bodies and Jesus was looking at them with love in His eyes and He was laughing with them! I was dumbfounded at what I was seeing. They all stopped about twenty feet from me and as I looked from the dogs to Jesus I saw that He was looking at me and he was smiling. When my eyes met His, it was as though they held me in place. His eyes were full of love and knowledge and I could feel it inside my being. The dogs hadn't even noticed me because they were too preoccupied with the presence of Jesus and then I saw Jesus lift His right arm up in the air and all of a sudden, all three dogs looked at me. And in an instant Petie was right in my face looking me right in the eyes and he began to talk to me. He did not actually talk with his mouth it was more of a mind communication and I could hear his thoughts in my mind. Almost my entire field of vision was taken up by the closeness of Petie's face. His eyes were right up close to mine and they seemed bigger than they normally were in life, and they seemed to look right into me.

Petie licked my face and said, "I love you and I miss you. Don't worry about me any longer because I am happy and safe because now, I am with Jesus. Say hi to mommy (My wife) and tell her that I love her and miss her. Tell her not to worry or grieve over me any longer because I am home, and I am very happy. Tell her that I want for nothing, because Jesus gives me everything I need". I realized that I was crying and I told him, "I love you and miss you too Petie" and then Petie took off running to play with Jesus again. Jesus was still watching me with that smile.

Duke came next in the same fashion as Petie; in an instant. And the strange thing was that I had not really been praying to see Petie or Duke. Duke had not once been in my mind during this whole ordeal of the past month. The first thing Duke asked me was, "Do you still remember me?" And I said, "Yes, I grew up with you". And then childhood memories flooded my mind. And I am ashamed to admit that I had not forgotten him, but that he had not been in my mind this entire time. It had been well over 30 years since he had passed and I only thought of him occasionally. Duke then asked, "Do you remember? Me and you grew up together; you as a young child and me as a puppy, and we did everything together" and I said, "How could I forget you?" He then licked me and said, "I love you very much, and we will be together again soon, and we will play together just like we used to do in life, right in this very spot" and I thought, "In life?" He then ran off and began to play with Jesus and Petie. During this whole experience, in between each dog I looked at Jesus and He was always watching me with that loving smile. I knew in my heart that He was getting the biggest kick out of watching me.

BJ came next and what he said I will never forget. He said, "I love you and miss you so much. Of all the humans that I knew in my life while I was on earth, I loved you the most because you were the only one I ever really completely trusted. You realize now, that you and I had a special relationship. Jesus blessed us both and He brought us together for His purpose and you also know now, what that purpose is". Then BJ licked me and his face became serious and he said, "Hold on to your faith and follow Jesus so that we will be together again in heaven. I will be waiting for you and I will see you soon. Remember, keep close to Jesus and never let go of your faith, and soon we will play in this very field together, all of us" and I told him, "I love you and I miss you so much, please don't go yet" he then kissed me again and he took off with Petie, Duke, and Jesus.

I then saw all three dogs running into the distance together jumping and playing and they were *laughing* like little children. And all of a sudden I realized in that moment, that all three dogs *knew* each other.

The Lord Jesus approached me while I was staring at my dogs running away and then we were face to face. His eyes were full of love and He looked at me as though He was proud of me. I then had another realization, that Jesus knew everything about me. He knew I would be saved and would belong to Him and He also knew that we would meet in this field. I knew that He was acutely aware of all my feelings, emotions, and doubts. And He knew that I had been mad with him, and it seemed to amuse Him.

Jesus then began to explain why He sent BJ to me, and why He took BJ from me. Jesus said, *"I wanted you to learn unconditional love and forgiveness from my dog. And I wanted you to learn to love me, and other humans, the same way you loved BJ. Everything belongs to me and everything comes back to me. Everything is a temporary gift and each gift has a purpose. Duke and BJ were made for only you, and Petie was made for your wife, and your sons. BJ and Petie were not made for your grandchildren"*.

I asked Jesus, "Why did you take so long to answer me?" And He replied, *"Steven, many people have wondered where their animals go after they have died, but no one has ever taken the time to seek the answer from me, but you did. Although I know many people love my animals, no one has really cared enough about them to find out. And many don't have enough faith to ask me. I would have told them if only they had asked. Your love for BJ was so strong that I was touched by it. And besides, I have really enjoyed listening to your prayers. You pray to me always, asking for more faith, but Steven you have faith because your determination to get an answer shows this. You just don't realize how much faith you really have".*

I asked Jesus "Why didn't you answer my prayers to keep BJ alive. I thought that you answered all prayers, *why* didn't you honor my prayers. Why Lord? You know how much pain his death has caused me. Are you punishing me?" And He explained to me, *"I sent BJ to you, in order to teach you some things that you need to know. Sometimes your prayers get in the way of your other prayers. Now Steven, didn't you pray for a dog that your grandchildren could love, pet, and be close to through their childhood? A dog to teach them love, morals, and values just like Duke did for you and Petie did for your two sons? You know your grandchildren could not be close to Petie or BJ because they were too dangerous for them to love."* And I said, "Yes but I wanted you to make Petie and BJ lovable for them. You made BJ love me, why couldn't you make BJ and Petie love them?" and Jesus answered, *"They were both too old for your grandchildren. They could not grow up with Petie and BJ, and I knew in your heart that you wanted your grandchildren to grow up with a dog. And you know that it had to be a young dog".*

He was right, that was in my heart but I didn't want to lose BJ either. I wanted my cake and eat it too, but I knew deep inside there was no other way, Jesus was right. And besides, a third dog would have never worked because it would have been too much on me and my wife. Jesus took Petie a year before BJ passed and I see now that there was a second reason God sent BJ to us. Not only was BJ sent to teach me how to love the Lord, but also to help cushion the blow of Petie's death. (In fact my wife and BJ had begun to draw closer to each other just before he passed. Love...love did it). I could feel in the eyes of Jesus that He was aware of my thoughts. Then Jesus looked at me as though He was looking into my soul, into my very being, and He asked me, *"Wasn't that what was really in your heart?"* and I could feel Him in my heart and I knew that there were no secrets that I could possibly hide from Him, and I bowed my head crying and said, "Yes Lord". He was right. My grand-children could never be close to BJ or Petie and they needed a young dog with the energy to match theirs. And yes, in my heart I wanted my grandchildren to learn love, loyalty, forgiveness, responsibility and all the things that growing up with a pet can do for a person. *I wanted* this more than *I needed* BJ.

Then I begged Him to take my pain away and He did. It was as if He gave me a whole different view, or a new knowledge of life and death. Jesus didn't say a word, I just felt His wisdom come into me and it opened my eyes and I realized that my dogs are a *part* or a *little piece of* God; just like we are. I knew that every creature in the universe was connected to Him and that only human beings have a choice to disconnect.

I knew then positively without a doubt, that all my pets were alive and in heaven and that they were in a far better place than here on earth with me. How could I not be happy for them? I knew now that they were happy, they were safe, and they had eternal life, but more importantly, I knew that they weren't just a pile of dust. I knew for a fact that they were alive...*forever*.

Knowing this took most of the pain away and especially knowing that I would see them again. Just knowing that I would be with them forever made me happy in a way that I cannot describe, and that knowledge or feeling *healed* me right then and there. After all; what better place to be, than in the arms of Jesus the creator? It was just like the Bible says; he wiped all my tears away in an instant. Then I asked Jesus where I was because my dogs had said they would see me here and I wanted to know where "here" was. Sometime earlier right after I was saved, Jesus took me to a beautiful mountain where there was an unbelievable sunset with indescribable colors. There was no sun, and I knew that it was the light that radiated from Jesus that was painting this particular sunset and that he had created that sunset just for me.

Jesus answered *"Steven, I know you love the mountains, the stars, and the sunsets. I know you love the outdoors and that you have always acknowledged that I created it. You have always believed in me, but you have never been close to me. But you know me now. Steven, this place is another one of your mansions."* (When I read the scripture in the Gospel about Jesus going to prepare mansions for us, I thought it was talking about houses! He told me that mansions were houses but they were also places that I loved on earth, only they were in heaven too, but much more beautiful. When in heaven, it is only a mere thought to be in any of our mansions).

Then Jesus said, *"BJ's mission is complete and his work is finished. He had to come back home to me because he is mine. I knew which prayer you really wanted in your heart which was a dog for your grandchildren. You prayed for a dog that they could grow up with because you wanted them to learn about love and forgiveness. And I have created an animal that can do this. So if you want to know what I'm like just look at a dog, because I made them just like me. They have unconditional love, unconditional forgiveness, and they are loyal. A dog will stay by your side until the end just like me. So you see Steven, your prayers got in the way of each other, but I knew which prayer you really wanted most. Did you not dedicate your grandchildren to me? I will teach them as I taught you. And I will guide you through the scriptures and show you of my love for all of my creatures. You will know for certain that your dogs come back to heaven. I send my creatures to teach man but many do not learn, due to their arrogance, but you are different; you learn because your mind is open to my word. Didn't I make you pray more and draw you closer to me through BJ's death? Why can't you love me like you loved BJ and in the same manner that BJ loved you...unconditionally. Why can't you love me like a dog; with unconditional love? I knew you and your wife before you were both born and I gave you both the gift of love for animals. I also gave you the gift of humor. Love and humor are my two greatest gifts. I want your grandchildren to have a dog that they can be close to, so that they may learn to love also. You want what I want. I have heard you talk to me but you thought I wasn't listening, but I was. I have been with you all along...you just didn't know it."*

Jesus then explained to me how important forgiveness was and that love and forgiveness go hand in hand. Then instantly my vision transformed. Jesus was on the cross and He was bloody and beaten. The cross was slowly turning around as if He wanted me to see every facet of His body. He wanted me to see all that man had done to Him on the cross, and yet he said that He *still forgave us*. It was brutal and horrible and I wanted to look away, and I tried to look away, but I couldn't. I could only stare dumbfounded. I began to cry and I could still hear Him speaking to me and He said, *"Steven, the last prayer that I asked while I hung on the cross was about forgiveness; I asked the Father to forgive them because they didn't know what they were doing. They were lost just like you were. If I had not said this prayer, the whole purpose of me coming to earth would have been void. All my words, my actions, and my gift of salvation that I brought with me for all men, would have been in vain. All my suffering through the crucifixion depended on that one prayer of forgiveness. You cannot enter heaven with any unforgiveness in your heart, and neither could I, and my animals teach this better than any of my other creations, including man. Men teach animals and animals teach men. They are connected. All things are connected, and they are connected to me. Now go to my word and I will show you what I say about my whole creation; all of it. Tell it to people so they will know and believe that there are no limits to my love. So that they will know that I love my animals too and that they come back to me. I have selected you to deliver this message. I will guide you and explain my words through the spirit."*

Then Jesus was right in front of me as before and He was beautiful and radiant once again. He stood back from me about five feet and I suddenly noticed that He was holding BJ in His arms petting him and they were both just looking at me. (This is the part I would later see again many times). I could see the unspeakable love in *both* of their eyes and it was as if they were one. BJ's white and black fur was radiant and he was very still and calm. His eyes were clear and shiny just like the eyes of Jesus and BJ had what looked like a "holy haircut". His fur looked *electrified* and as I stared at his fur I realized that his fur was *alive*. His fur was *alive*! And I could see knowledge in BJ's eyes, that I *knew far surpassed my own*. I could *feel* it. BJ no longer had that look of sadness, or that questioning look of, "Am I loved?" He had a look of *complete and total serenity*. That is the only word I can think of to describe what I saw in his face and his eyes. Serenity and love radiated from him and I could feel it wash over me from my head to my feet. I knew that it all came from Jesus. And a revelation, or a realization hit me like a ton of bricks. BJ was a different animal; he was not the dog I knew on earth and I actually felt inferior to him! Immediately a scripture came into my mind: *"They shall not hurt nor destroy in all my holy mountain: for the earth shall be full of the knowledge of the LORD, as the waters cover the sea."*

(Isaiah 11:9) It dawned on me that BJ was full of the Lord's knowledge! I knew that he was in his glorified body because God had renewed him. Jesus had given him eternal life. My BJ was in heaven and there were no more doubts at all in my mind. He did exist...forever. And finally, all the pain and grief were gone. But don't get me wrong, I still miss him and I always will until we are reunited in heaven. Then BJ jumped from the arms of Jesus and disappeared. Jesus had answered my prayers in a much better way than I could ever imagine.

I was dumbfounded for a few moments. Jesus and I just stared at each other and I knew then that I had to let BJ go and move on with my life because he was no longer mine. And as a matter of fact, I knew that he had never really been mine. I felt Jesus reading my mind and I asked Jesus, "When and how will I find another dog, how will I know? What kind of dog should I get? Where do I look?" And Jesus answered, *"I will tell you when it is time and I will show you which dog to get for them. You will know. And remember Steven, love and forgiveness are the keys to heaven because they are the same. Tell people of this vision and tell them of my great love for all my creation. And Steven, try to be more like a dog."* (I knew it! God had a sense of humor!)

90

Then all of a sudden a bright light began to radiate from Jesus. And I saw light radiating and shooting like pulsars from the holes in His hands and feet where seconds before they had been bloody, and nailed to the cross. And I knew in my mind that He was showing me his Glory. I realized that this was only a small part of His Glory. I knew that if He had shown me anymore of His glory than what He did, I would have died.

Then I was back in my living room and I was full of the spirit. My pain and grief for BJ had diminished. My mind was clear and focused and I knew without a doubt, that BJ was in the hands of the greatest owner in the universe. I knew he was happy and was loved far beyond anything that I could ever possibly imagine. There was nothing that I could ever attempt to give him that would even compare to what he had now. I also knew then, that he was home in heaven and safe in the arms of Jesus, where I would be someday. I knew that my dogs were in heaven waiting for me. There was no doubt in my mind any longer where BJ was and I was overwhelmed with joy.

Jesus told me that His last prayer was forgiveness and so I looked in the Bible and sure enough, it was His *last* prayer! How many times had I read that verse and never even realized that it was His last prayer before He died. The last words of Jesus before he died on the cross were, *"it is finished"* but it would not have been finished if not for that one all important prayer of forgiveness. He had to forgive His persecutors in order for the Father to receive Him into heaven.

Jesus said we are all born from spirit into flesh, and that man must be born *again* into the spirit (saved and baptized) but not animals, because they don't sin. Their spirits are different and so are the spirits of angels.

There are three facts about redemption that Jesus showed me:

1. Man *needs* redemption.
2. Animals *don't need* redemption.
3. And there *is no redemption* for angels.

Knowing the fact that animals are sinless and don't need redemption, and that angels can't be redeemed, helped me to understand how desperate we need Jesus as our savoir. Animals have a free ride and angels are damned if they sin just once, but we have a choice. It is a simple choice, but for many it is hard. What we need, animals *don't* need. And what we need, angels *can't* have. And what we need, all we have to do is ask for it. Realizing this helped me to forgive and love my enemies much easier, because now I see my enemies and all people in a different light. And I learned all this from a little lost dog. Jesus is amazing. Thank you Jesus!

Chapter 12

My Wife's Dream

"...blessed are they that hear the word of God,
and keep it." -Luke 11:28

L ike I stated, I prayed for three weeks determined to see BJ one more time because I needed to know if he was in heaven with Jesus, or simply just dust in the ground. Finally, after I had my second vision I told my wife.

She then told me that she had a dream of BJ *the day after* he died. She did not tell me until after I had told her of my second vision. I asked her why she did not tell me about her dream and she said that she knew I would be upset and did not want to bring it up. She knew I was praying to see BJ but had received no answer. And yet, she saw BJ in a dream given by God, and hadn't prayed about BJ at all. My wife knew if she told me of her dream that I would be mad with Jesus so she wanted to wait a while, until I was somewhat over BJ (She and Jesus both know I am hard headed. Jesus has his hands full working on me!)

When I told my wife about my vision we compared our descriptions of BJ and we both saw him as a young and vibrant looking animal. His black and white fur was very vivid and looked almost electrified. My wife said that BJ's white fur was whiter than anything she had ever seen. She said it was a holy white and that his hair looked as though it had been cut and manicured by a holy barber and I saw the same thing. I reminded her that BJ was at the groomers not quite a month before he passed. And we always had the groomer shave his fur close like a crew cut. His hair was short when he passed, but in her dream and in my vision, his fur was a longer medium length. And we both agreed that when we saw his fur, it looked electrified and alive. In her dream my wife was sitting on our swing in the back yard and she saw BJ by the picnic table; one of his favorite places to lie down. My wife told me that she looked at BJ and said, "Oh BJ, you are so pretty, and so young looking." She said that he was standing by the picnic table with his chest stuck out like he was proud of his new body. My wife said that he was smiling and she could see his teeth which she said looked brilliantly white. She turned to tell us to look at BJ standing over by the picnic table, but when she turned to tell us, she realized we were not there. And when she turned back to look at BJ again, he was gone. She woke up then.

She said that BJ did not speak to her, he only smiled as though he was saying, "Look at me! Look at my new body. I'm young and happy, and I have no pain. I'm with Jesus".

Chapter 13

Jesus Sends Jasper

"Thou sendest forth thy spirit, they are created:
and thou renewest the face of the earth."
-Psalm 104:30

For two weeks after BJ died, I searched the internet for a Shih Tzu thinking I could find one just like BJ. I searched for about an hour a day and I saw abused pets that needed homes, and all it did was make me miss BJ even more. I thought that Jesus would show me the one He wanted me to have through the pictures on the internet. But Jesus remained quiet.

One day while I was on the internet I saw a Shih Tzu and he was in a shelter several counties away. It was about a sixty mile drive so I decided to go take a look at the dog. You know, just a look. I had just arrived at the shelter when my wife called me on the cell phone and she asked me where I was. I knew if I told her where I was she would think I was losing it over BJ. So I sheepishly said, "Well... uh." She asked me again where I was and I knew I couldn't tell her anything different other than the truth. When I told her where I was she said, "I think you need therapy." Yes, she was absolutely right but I wouldn't admit it. I just said "Well...I just wanted to look at this dog because it's a Shih Tzu, just like BJ. You should see him, he looks just like BJ." She gave me direct orders to get home immediately and do not bring any dogs home with me.

I did get to see the dog but it was not the same as BJ. He looked a lot like him, but it wasn't BJ. Have you ever been like that? You know that you can't replace an individual, yet grief drives you to try. On the way home I realized what I was doing to myself. I could never replace the unique spirit that was BJ. God had made him unique and there was only one BJ. But sometimes when we are grieving and desperate, we try. Finally, I let it go and gave it back to Jesus. I didn't need therapy, I needed Jesus. And finally Jesus delivered me from *myself*.

The next day I was watching television and a commercial came on the screen asking for donations to help abused animals. Sad music was playing and the screen was showing many different abused animals. Then I saw one that looked exactly like BJ. He had a missing eye and he was very sad looking. It made me sad and I began to realize how lonely the house was without BJ. I began to pray to Jesus. Then Jesus spoke to me. *"I want you to get a dog that is in danger of being put down. You may think that saving one animal's life doesn't matter, but to me it does. Go to the dog pound and I will show you which dog I have sent to you."* And I said "But Lord, how will I know which dog is for me. Will it be another Shih Tzu?" and He answered, *"You will know"*.

So I told my wife what the Lord had said and we got in our car and I began to drive for the shelter in the next county but just as we got within a few yards of the old road that led to our local shelter, which I had forgotten about, my wife said, "Turn on this road." And so I whipped the wheel to the right and we went down the road towards the local shelter. There are two dog shelters in our local area and they are both on the same road. One is in our own county and the other one is in the adjoining county which is only about two miles away. I had forgotten about the one in our county because the city had constructed a new highway and our dog shelter had been bypassed leaving it setting back off the road and out of site. I didn't even think of that one and it was only minutes away.

Little did I know Jesus was at work using my wife to complete His plan.

When we entered the dog shelter I still had my reservations and I thought that maybe we were at the wrong animal shelter and that we should have gone to the other one. My wife had diverted me from my mission and I really didn't want to stay there too long because I wanted to get down the road to the other shelter before someone took the dog that was supposed to be mine. I had only turned onto that road because my wife had told me to, and due to the fact that she had caught me by surprise telling me to turn at the last moment. You men know what I'm talking about, you get used to listening to orders from the boss; your wife, and you immediately do what she says. We entered the shelter and walked over to the front desk. We briefly talked to the young lady behind the counter and she called someone to take us through the shelter to look at the animals. An older lady came from the back and she led us through the door that entered into the cage area. There was a long hallway that was lined with cages on each side. I thought, "Ok Jesus, show us which dog you have chosen for us if this is the place."

As we walked down the isle I noticed that all the dogs were backing up in their cages as if someone were scolding them. And some were barking briefly but they acted as though they were not interested in us, and that struck me as strange. Finally as we got to the very last cage on the left, I saw *three* dogs together in a cage. (There are many things that happen in the Bible in three's). Two were standing back just observing us but the other one was right up to the cage jumping up and putting his paws on the cage. He was barking and whining at me and my wife, and it was almost as if he was saying, "Here I am. Here I am." And at that moment the spirit must have hit me and my wife at the same time, because we both told the lady, "That's the one we want". We said it in unison. My wife and I both looked at each other and smiled because we knew the spirit had hit us both, but we didn't say anything to each other until we were alone. It was a confirmation of the spirit because we had both known at the same instant without any doubts. Jesus had spoken to both of us. The lady got the dog and took us into a receiving room where she could let the dog off the leash and we could inspect him.

My mind was made up because I knew this was the dog that Jesus had picked out and my wife agreed. The lady left us alone for a few minutes and my wife and I both agreed that the Lord had chosen this dog because we both had felt the same thing. I could see the spirit all over the dog and he was acting like he knew us. The dog was a male Cairn terrier, mixed with Chihuahua and he looked like a red fox. His fur was a brown and golden color with reddish tips on the ends and he had long slim legs like Petie. His face had a small beard and moustache just like BJ and his eyes were big black, and round, just like BJ. How awesome is God?

When the lady came back we told her we definitely wanted this dog so we asked her what his name was and she said that he didn't have a name. She informed us that he had arrived as a young puppy and that he was five months old now and that he hadn't been named yet. It was perfect but our only fear was; how is he with children? We asked the lady if he was child friendly and she said she wasn't sure but she thought he was. But I *knew* he would be good with kids simply because Jesus picked him out. And so, we took our new gift from Jesus home with us that day.

To our surprise he was already house trained! How convenient. (We thanked Jesus for that because He knew we were too old to fool with that mess). When my two grandchildren came over and saw him for the first time they fell in love; all three of them. The dog and the children bonded immediately and my granddaughter wanted to know his name. We told her that he didn't have a name, so we gave her the honor of naming the dog. (My granddaughter is four years old and she goes to church and she knows Jesus). So she came up with a name and can you believe it; she named him Jasper. That's one of the colors of God's throne.

If you could only see how my grandchildren and Jasper play together you would agree with us that it was the perfect dog picked by the Lord Jesus to come into our lives. And when my youngest grandson comes over, Jasper treats him gentle. Jasper knows he is just a young child…his spirit knows. And my youngest grandson will grow up with Jasper too. Jasper lives here with us, but it's obvious who his best friends are; the grandchildren. There is no doubt in our mind that Jesus gave us this special dog as a gift of love for us and our grandchildren, and that assurance grows stronger every day.

They all play together and they wear each other out. On several occasions we have found them all in a pile asleep where they have worn each other out. Jasper cries sometimes when they are gone and if you mention their names to him he will go stand at the window and whine.

We love him dearly and I know that Duke, Petie and BJ are in heaven playing with Jesus…forever. Our new dog Jasper gives us love and we love him in return. And we know that Jesus also gave us a dog that reminds us of our Petie and our BJ to help with our loss, and to help us remember our beloved pets that are now in heaven with Jesus. They are safe and are waiting for us to be united with them in heaven. Oh yea, and Jasper will be there with us too!

Jesus later told me, *"Your mansions are in heaven and they are everything that you love on earth only much more. And when you are in heaven, all you need do is think of them and you are there and your pets can be with you in your mansions. They can be with you, your wife and with me all at the same time. There are no limits in heaven and there are no limits with love. You see Steven, heaven is love."*

PART III

"And E-li'-sha prayed, and said, LORD, I pray thee, open his eyes, that he may see. And the LORD opened the eyes of the young man; and he saw; and, behold, the mountain was full of horses and chariots of fire round about E-li'-sha." -2 Kings 6:17

Chapter 14

King Solomon's Wisdom

"Who knoweth the spirit of man that goeth upward, and the spirit of the beast that goeth downward to the earth?" -Ecclesiastes 3:21

*D*o animals go to heaven? Many people have asked this question throughout the ages but yet none have really taken the time to ask Jesus. King Solomon asked the same question, but only to himself. Where do the spirits of animals go? Do they go to heaven or do they just die and turn to dust and go into the earth and that's the end of them?

"I said in mine heart concerning the estate of the sons of men, that God might manifest them, and that they might see that they themselves are beasts. For that which befalleth the sons of

men befalleth beasts; even one thing befalleth them: as the one dieth, so dieth the other; yea, they have all one breath; so that a man hath no preeminence above a beast: for all is vanity. All go unto one place; all are of the dust, and all turn to dust again. Who knoweth the spirit of man that goeth upward, and the spirit of the beast that goeth downward to the earth?"
(Ecclesiastes 3:18-21)

King Solomon is asking a *question*.....not making a statement. If you notice there is a *question* mark at the end of the verse, not a period. He asks, "Who knows?" Many people who read the Bible do not notice this question mark. King Solomon was pondering the age old question, not making a statement. And if you notice the last sentence in the verse above, he says that beasts *do have spirits*. Here is more proof that animals do have spirits.

In the verse above, King Solomon describes our realistic *equality* with animals when he states that we are no better than animals and that man has no preeminence above a beast. In fact we are worse than they are...we need salvation and they don't. And lastly, King Solomon says that we all have one breath, which we know is God's *breath*. And he states that he is aware that the bodies of all men and beasts turn to dust, but he still wonders where the spirit of the animal goes.

Perhaps, King Solomon had a dog, or a horse, or maybe a cat that he cared a lot about and it passed on. Why else would he be pondering this question. Something had to happen to make him ask this particular question.

People have always owned animals and have grown close to them whether they were house pets, beasts of burden, or any other animal. They loved their animals too, the same as we do and as a matter of fact, some cultures have put animals on a pedestal. King Solomon and many other ancient people have asked this age old question; just as we do today.

Did it ever cross your mind, that it is quite possible, that maybe even Adam and Eve had a pet or a favorite animal that they were close to. Adam and Eve had to use animals to do their work, so surely they had some feelings towards some of them. And I am sure that they grieved too, whenever their pets passed on. But perhaps they knew something that we don't know today; the fact that animals have spirits, and that they do go back to Jesus.

"I know that, whatsoever God doeth, it shall be for ever:..." (Ecclesiastes 3:14)

Here in the verse above, King Solomon states that whatever God makes; it is made to last forever. And we have already established that God made everything in the universe. So it stands to reason that this includes all animals, plants, stars, planets, men, etc. This leads us to the fact that if God makes everything to last forever, and animals are sinless, and that they do have spirits, and God preserves them; then there is no other place for animals to go except *heaven.*

Chapter 15

We Brought Animals Into Sin

"The wolf also shall dwell with the lamb..."
-Isaiah 11:6

Man brought animals and everything on this earth into sin, because animals did not sin, we did. Animals cannot sin and therefore they have no need for redemption, a Bible, or a church.

The verse below states that we corrupted ourselves and all of creation, due to our fall into sin nature. The Apostle Paul states in the book of Romans,

> *"For the creature was made subject to vanity, not willingly, but by reason of him who hath subjected the same in hope. Because the creature itself also shall be delivered from the bondage of*

corruption into the glorious liberty of the chil-

dren of God. For we know that the whole cre-

ation groaneth and travaileth in pain together

until now. And not only they, but ourselves also,

which have the firstfruits of the Spir'-it, even we

ourselves groan within ourselves, waiting for

the adoption to wit, the redemption of our body."

(Romans 8:20-23)

Look closely at the verse above and notice that it says, for the creature (animals) were subjected to sin by us and that they (animals) will be *delivered* from corruption (sin), into the *"...glorious liberty of the children of god"* (men). *We* are the Children of God. The "glorious liberty" that he is talking about is to be free of this sin curse and to be in heaven with Jesus, not to mention having eternal life with glorified bodies. Bottom line...animals will also be delivered from sin and return to heaven with us. Look at the last half of the verse. The Apostle Paul says the *"...the whole of creation groans"* in this corrupted world, *together*. We all suffer alike and we all suffer together due to the sin nature, and the corruption brought on by sin.

Paul states that we have the *"firstfruits"* of the spirit. This means that animals have spirits but we have the *"firstfruits"* of the spirit. Yes, we are more special than the creature, but this verse shows that animals have spirits too, and they will be liberated from this corruption just as we will. Which can only mean one thing; they have to go to heaven. The Hebrew word *"firstfruits"* actually means the first part of the harvest and so, it simply states that all creatures are part of the harvest, but that man is first; or at the top of the list.

This means that we all, including animals (creatures), are waiting for redemption; waiting to be free of this sin curse. Look at the words, *"...waiting for the adoption to wit"*. This simply means we are all waiting to be adopted back into the family of Christ where we all belong, both men and creatures alike.

Paul states that, *"...for the creature was made subject to vanity."* Which simply means that animals were brought into sin due to our vanity and our arrogance (Or closed minds and lack of faith).

> *"That in the dispensation of the fullness of times*
> *he might gather together in one all things in*
> *Christ, both which are in heaven, and which*
> *are on earth; even in him." (Ephesians 1:10)*

113

In the above verse, Paul states that God will bring all of His blessed creation back to him. Animals and people shall live together just as they did in the Garden of Eden. If as stated, Jesus gathers all things that are in heaven and earth in him, then why would animals not be included? I don't see anywhere in the verse above that says he will gather everything except animals. So therefore it stands to reason that God will not only gather humans, but *all* things that are on the earth and in heaven.

The Bible tells us that animals are in heaven and that they will also be here on the new earth. And here's something to ponder, it says all things in *heaven* and earth. This includes the angels, the heavenly beings, and all the heavenly animals. We will see them and know them too.

> *"The wolf also shall dwell with the lamb, and the leopard shall lie down with the kid; and the calf and the young lion and the fatling together; and a little child shall lead them. And the cow and the bear shall feed; their young ones shall lie down together; and the lion shall eat straw like the ox. And the sucking child shall play on the hole of the asp, and the weaned child shall put his hand on the cockatrice' den. They shall not*

hurt nor destroy in all my holy mountain: for the
earth shall be full of the knowledge of the LORD,
as the waters cover the sea." (Isaiah 11:6-9)

God has bound men and animals together on this earth since the beginning of creation. Isaiah states in the verse above, that animals and humans will be in the new kingdom of God here on earth living together in harmony, which definitely shows that the earth will be renewed and will once again be a Garden of Eden. So it stands to reason that your pets and other animals will be in heaven. Your pets and your saved loved ones shall be in heaven with the Lord, forever and ever.

AMEN.

And every once in a while, God allows me to see Jesus holding BJ in that beautiful field of heaven, when I shut my eyes and ask.

Epilogue

About three months after I had my visions I composed a small message about my vision. I wanted to witness my experience in church because Jesus had told me to tell people about his message that He revealed to me in my visions. I tried to deliver my message three times but it didn't work out. I was rather relieved because I don't like to stand in front of people and talk. So I told Jesus that He couldn't be mad at me because I had tried to do it, but no one wanted to hear about a dog and therefore I was off the hook.

About a week later after trying to deliver the message that Jesus had given me, I was feeling a little guilty for not telling people like Jesus had told me to do, even though it wasn't my fault. I was in my living room praying and I was telling Jesus that somebody ought to write a book telling people that animals go to heaven. And Jesus said, "Somebody is going to write a book about animals going to heaven" and I asked, "Really! Who?" because I really wanted to read that book! And Jesus said, "You are" and I said, "Me?!" And I told the Lord that I didn't know the first thing about writing or publishing a book. I had always prayed and asked Jesus to show me where I fit in with His plans, but he has never shown me. I would never have guessed that He would instruct me to write a book.

Jesus told me that He would direct me and help me to accomplish this task. He then began to show me the scriptures that He wanted me to use and He gave me the wisdom to understand these verses that I have quoted in this book. I had read several of these very scriptures at various times before, but I never really caught their real meaning. This was due to the fact that I was reading them with a closed mind. At that time when I read them, I was only thinking about humans, and I had missed the true message about His total love for all of His creation.

When I was almost finished writing this book something strange happened to me. I was reading my Bible and I dropped it, and when I picked it up it was open to Psalm 96 and I happened to glance down at verse 12. And there on the top left page it read: *"Let the field be joyful, and all that is therein; then shall all the trees of the wood rejoice"*.

Maybe the Lord was telling me that this was the beautiful field I had been in with my beloved pets.

To My Wife

B efore I met my wife, I prayed to Jesus and I asked that He would give me a God fearing woman. One who I could trust to help me for life. One who I could trust to raise my children with morals and values. And one who would be with me through everything. When my wife and I met we knew it was God's will. When we were married we knew that it was a holy union. We have been married for over 30 years. God answered my prayers.

Work Cited

King James Version of the Holy Bible. Large Compact Edition. Published by Holman Bible Publishers, Nashville Tennessee. Copyright 1998. Mass Market Edition 005405430

Random House Webster's College Dictionary. Copyright 2000 by Random House, Inc. April 2000 Second Revised.

About the Author

I was born in Houston, Texas.

I have resided in West Virginia for 30 years. My wife and I have been married for 30 years. As a young man, I was active in my church. I sang in the choir, and was an acolyte, and flag bearer.

I was a Boy Scout as a child.

I was a swimming instructor and I have given guitar lessons. I play the guitar and the banjo.

I spent four years in the Navy. I was Honor man of my boot camp company and I was a Communications Technician. I Graduated from Shepherd University in 2000 with an RBA in psychology at the age of 47. I was inducted into two honor societies and won two grants. I also had two pieces of literature published in the college book, Sans Merci.

I am retired with 30 years of government service.

I have two wonderful sons, and three grandchildren, one dog, and a bird that barks like a dog.

CPSIA information can be obtained
at www.ICGtesting.com
Printed in the USA
BVHW040440090622
639311BV00001B/32